HUMAN PERFORMANCE

Volume 10, Number 2, 1997

SPECIAL ISSUE: ORGANIZATIONAL CITIZENSHIP BEHAVIOR

Walter C. Borman and Stephan J. Motowidlo, *Guest Editors*

HUMAN PERFORMANCE, *10*(2), 67–69

INTRODUCTION

Organizational Citizenship Behavior and Contextual Performance

We are delighted to offer *Human Performance* readers seven articles focused on organizational citizenship behavior (OCB), contextual performance, and related concepts. We think you will agree that they make an important contribution to this burgeoning literature.

This topic (we will refer to it generically as contextual performance) seems to be generating considerable interest recently. The amount of research and discussion in the literature regarding contextual performance is definitely on the rise. Why might this be? Our take on it is that contextual performance is a very timely concept for the organization of today (and into the foreseeable future). More is expected of organizations' employees as global competition continues to require greater effort and productivity. Team-based structures call out for more cooperation between organization members. Increasing emphasis on customer service means employees must extend more interpersonal effort toward customers, as well as representing the organization favorably to current and potential customers. As "jobs" become a less relevant concept, replaced by fields of work or dynamic task force structures, employee adaptability and a willingness to engage in self-development to help the organization remain competitive becomes more and more important. These and related trends focus attention on contextual performance.

Now we comment briefly on each of the articles. Motowidlo, Borman, and Schmit describe a theory of job performance that includes a distinction between task and contextual performance. Motowidlo et al. assert that the effects of cognitive ability and personality on job performance are not so much direct as mediated by knowledge, skills, and work habits. An important prediction that arises out of this theory is that contextual performance is more strongly associated with personality variables, whereas task performance is more strongly associated with cognitive ability.

Organ offers a delightful retrospective on the OCB construct. It turns out the original OCB measure was developed by asking managers what they liked their employees to do on the job that they could not be "forced to do." Organ provides a useful commentary on definitional issues regarding OCB, contextual performance, and the like. He also speculates on how these concepts might be most advantageously positioned to describe OCB in today's organizations where employees are asked to do "whatever it takes."

Borman and Motowidlo review research results confirming part of the framework proposed by Motowidlo et al. Personality is related to contextual performance, and there is some evidence that this link is stronger than the link between personality and task performance. It is suggested that meta-analytic results showing moderate correlations between some personality constructs and job performance might be reinterpreted. Personality may be predicting the contextual elements of overall performance.

Penner has been interested in helping behavior in the context of volunteering. The article by Penner, Midili, and Kegelmeyer brings this personality/social psychological perspective into an organizational setting. Their study demonstrates that focused personality constructs measuring a prosocial personality orientation successfully predict OCB. Penner et al. also propose an interesting model hypothesizing that engaging in OCB affects one's self-concept toward a role identity as a good organizational citizen, in turn leading to enduring levels of OCB.

Podsakoff and Mackenzie report on the research that is arguably most important in this area, studying the links between OCB and organizational effectiveness. There have been logical and conceptual reasons to believe that OCB is associated with organizational effectiveness, but establishing an empirical linkage is very important. Work that Podsakoff and his colleagues are doing does show such a relation.

The articles by George and Jones and by Speir and Frese are both concerned with the effects of the organizational environment on contextual performance. In particular, George and Jones explore the environmental conditions that either encourage or constrain organizational members' contextual performance. These include individuals' self-efficacy, organizational culture, company policies, and reward systems. Speir and Frese argue that personal initiative is a special element of contextual performance. Their notion is that self-efficacy is enhanced in settings where the worker has some control over the environment and the job is sufficiently complex to offer challenges and that self-efficacy is in turn important in the expression of initiative. These two contributions are important because they explore an additional antecedent to contextual performance beyond job attitudes and individual differences.

Together, these articles describe ideas about contextual performance, OCB, and similar patterns of behavior that have been developed by scholars working from quite different research traditions. One of the most exciting things about this for us is that it seems that the different research traditions are converging on the same notion—that besides formal job requirements, other patterns of behavior are also critical for organizational effectiveness and survival. These other patterns of behavior have been relatively ignored until recently, but now scholars are trying to define them, determine exactly why and how they are important for organizations, and identify their antecedents. Our hope is that results of these research efforts, described by articles in this special issue of *Human Performance,* will make it possible to develop new conceptual and practical tools for managing these important behaviors and in that way enhance human performance and organizational effectiveness.

Walter C. Borman and Stephan J. Motowidlo
Guest Editors

HUMAN PERFORMANCE, *10*(2), 71–83

A Theory of Individual Differences in Task and Contextual Performance

Stephan J. Motowidlo
Human Resource Research Center
University of Florida

Walter C. Borman
Department of Psychology
University of South Florida

Mark J. Schmit
Payless ShoeSource

This article describes a theory of job performance that assumes that job performance is behavioral, episodic, evaluative, and multidimensional. It defines job performance as the aggregated value to the organization of the discrete behavioral episodes that an individual performs over a standard interval of time. It uses the distinction between task and contextual performance to begin to identify and define underlying dimensions of the behavioral episodes that make up the performance domain. The theory predicts that individual differences in personality and cognitive ability variables, in combination with learning experiences, lead to variability in knowledge, skills, and work habits that mediate effects of personality and cognitive ability on job performance. An especially important aspect of this theory is that it predicts that the kinds of knowledge, skills, work habits, and traits that are associated with task performance are different from the kinds that are associated with contextual performance.

Selection research has paid more attention to predictors of performance than it has to the performance construct itself (Campbell, 1990). This is ironic because the logic of selection research puts the performance construct first; job performance is the engine presumed to drive the development and validation of predictors.

We do have sophisticated technologies for job analysis, and they serve well to identify important tasks that must be performed on the job, human attributes likely

---

Requests for reprints should be sent to Stephan J. Motowidlo, Human Resource Research Center, 229 Business Building, University of Florida, Gainsville, FL 32611–7165.

to be important for job success, and patterns of behavior that differentiate effective from ineffective performers. They guide selection research by pointing to predictor constructs that might account for useful portions of the criterion domain in specific jobs or job families to which the job analyses are applied. They do not, however, describe general and theoretically satisfying models of job performance.

As Campbell, Gasser, and Oswald (1996) pointed out, general models or theories of job performance might have two broad themes. One is the dimensional structure of the performance domain. This theme involves efforts to identify and define categories of job performance that are broadly applicable to all jobs. The second theme is the causal pattern of relations between antecedents of job performance and its various dimensional components. This involves efforts to identify factors that explain variability in job performance and to show how they are related to each other in a causal sequence.

Our article describes a theory of job performance that attempts to incorporate both of these themes. We organized the article into three major sections. First, we present our fundamental assumptions about job performance. From these assumptions, we define job performance as the aggregated value to the organization of the discrete behavioral episodes that an individual performs over a standard interval of time. Second, we argue that the distinction between task and contextual performance (Borman & Motowidlo, 1993) is useful for identifying and defining underlying dimensions of the behavioral episodes that make up the performance domain. And third, we present a theory of individual differences in task and contextual performance. Our theory predicts that individual differences in personality and cognitive ability variables, in combination with learning experiences, lead to variability in knowledge, skills, and work habits that mediate effects of personality and cognitive ability on job performance. An especially important aspect of this theory is that it predicts that the kinds of knowledge, skills, work habits, and traits that are associated with task performance are different from the kinds that are associated with contextual performance.

BASIC ASSUMPTIONS ABOUT JOB PERFORMANCE

Starting from the conventional wisdom that job performance is essentially the degree to which an individual helps the organization reach its goals (Campbell, 1983), we assume that job performance is behavioral, episodic, evaluative, and multidimensional.

Performance Is a Behavioral Construct

Behavior, performance, and results are not the same things. Behavior is what people do while at work. Performance is behavior with an evaluative component, behavior that can be evaluated as positive or negative for individual or organizational effectiveness. Results are states or conditions of people or things that are changed by performance and consequently either contribute to or detract from organizational goal accomplishment. Results are the route through which an individual's performance helps or hinders an organization in reaching its goals, and this is what makes it appealing to focus on results when considering individual performance.

There are two important reasons, however, why a performance model should focus on behavior instead of results. First, states or conditions of things or people that are changed by performance are also affected by other factors not under the individual performer's control. Without adjustments for these extraneous factors, the apparent results of an individual's performance do not faithfully represent his or her own contribution to organizational goals. Second, a behavioral focus is necessary to develop a psychological understanding of selection processes and apply the full range of psychological principles and tools to the problem of prediction most fruitfully.

Performance Behavior Is Episodic

From one perspective, work behavior is a continuous stream that flows on seamlessly as people spend time at work. During the course of an 8-hr work day, however, people do many things that neither help nor hinder the organization accomplish its goals. Such behaviors have no effect on their performance. Thus, streams of work behavior are punctuated by occasions when people do something that does make a difference in relation to organizational goals and these are the behavioral episodes that make up the domain of job performance.

This raises the question of how the beginnings and endings of behavioral episodes in the performance domain might be identified so that performance episodes can be distinguished from the rest of the behavioral stream that is not relevant for organizational goals. Studies by Newtson and his colleagues (Newtson, 1973; Newtson, Engquist, & Bois, 1977) support the idea that when people observe an individual's behavior, they naturally segment it into discrete units to process social information. Newtson et al. (1977) argued that people perceive behavior as a series of coherent action units separated by breakpoints that define their beginnings and endings. Furthermore, perceivers can generally agree where the breakpoints are, although there is some flexibility about their location in the behavioral stream depending in part on perceivers' purposes and situational factors.

Performance Behavior Episodes Are Evaluative

Following Campbell (1990), our model presumes that only behavioral episodes that make a difference to organizational goal accomplishment are part of the performance domain. It also presumes that they vary widely according to their organizational contributions. The performance domain embraces behaviors that further the organization's goals dramatically as well as behaviors that further its goals only modestly. It also embraces behaviors that have negative effects and behaviors that have positive effects for organizational goal accomplishment. Thus, behavioral episodes in the performance domain have varying contribution values for the organization that range from slightly to extremely positive for behaviors that help organizational goal accomplishment and from slightly to extremely negative for behaviors that hinder organizational goal accomplishment.

Our model assumes that organizations have goals, but we acknowledge that the goals are not necessarily known or agreed upon by all organizational members. Also, organizations frequently have multiple goals that are unrelated to each other. As a result, specific events that enhance the accomplishment of some goals might have no effect on the accomplishment of others and even detract from the accomplishment of still others.

Despite these complexities, two lines of evidence suggest it is still reasonable to think about behavioral episodes according to their contribution to organizational goal accomplishment. First, when people are asked to describe critical incidents portraying unusually effective or ineffective work behaviors, they are generally able to produce them (Flanagan, 1954). More significantly, when asked to judge critical incidents for their overall level of effectiveness, they can do this with enough agreement to justify using specific critical incidents as anchors on behaviorally anchored rating scales. Second, when people are presented with brief scenarios describing problem situations on the job and asked to judge the effectiveness of alternative means of handling them, they can do this with enough agreement to distinguish reliably between more and less effective approaches (e.g., Motowidlo, Dunnette, & Carter, 1990). Thus, it is possible to identify behavioral episodes that are regarded as more or less organizationally desirable and to scale the degree to which they are organizationally desirable with enough precision to distinguish between them.

The Performance Domain Is Behaviorally Multidimensional

The aggregated contribution value of an individual's behavioral episodes over a standard interval of time represents the net worth of that individual's behavior to the organization during that time interval. It is that person's overall job performance. What makes it possible to accumulate information about all the behavioral episodes in the domain to form a single performance construct is that they can all be scaled according to a common metric—contribution value. When expressed this way in terms of total utility for organizational goal accomplishment, job performance is unidimensional.

However, there are many different kinds of behaviors that would advance or hinder organizational goals and lumping them all together produces a psychologically intractable hodge-podge. The aggregated contribution values for different incumbents can be meaningfully compared, but the behavioral episodes attached to them are too heterogeneous to allow meaningful comparisons between the overall behavioral patterns performed by different incumbents.

This creates a dilemma. We want to predict aggregated contribution value, but the behavioral substrate of this utility construct is too much of a jumble to offer clues about personal characteristics that might be related to it. If we already have some particular personal characteristics in mind, such as intelligence or conscientiousness, we can assess their relations with job performance as an aggregated contribution value. If, however, we want to deduce personal characteristics that might subsequently prove to be related to job performance, the aggregated contribution value by itself cannot guide us.

The solution to this dilemma is to organize the performance domain into behaviorally homogeneous categories and aggregate contribution values of behavioral episodes separately in each category. Then the efforts of selection research should be directed to the prediction of multiple criteria simultaneously, each representing the aggregated contribution value of behavioral episodes in one category.

TASK PERFORMANCE AND CONTEXTUAL PERFORMANCE

One way to develop behavioral categories is according to the reasons that behavioral episodes either contribute to or detract from organizational goal accomplishment. In fact, this is the basis for our distinction between task performance and contextual performance (Borman & Motowidlo, 1993). The reason task behaviors are organizationally desirable or undesirable is very different from the reason contextual behaviors are organizationally desirable or undesirable. We also expect that antecedents of task performance are different from antecedents of contextual performance (Motowidlo & Van Scotter, 1994).

There are two types of task performance. One consists of activities that transform raw materials into the goods and services that are the organization's products. They include activities such as selling merchandise in a retail store, operating a production machine in a manufacturing plant, teaching in a school, performing surgery in a hospital, and cashing checks in a bank. A second type of task performance consists of activities that service and maintain the technical core by replenishing its supply of raw materials; distributing its finished products; or providing important planning, coordination, supervising, or staff functions that enable it to function effectively and efficiently. Thus, task performance bears a direct relation to the organization's technical core, either by executing its technical processes or by maintaining and servicing its technical requirements.

Contextual performance does not contribute through the organization's core technical processes but it does maintain the broader organizational, social, and psychological environment in which the technical core must function. It includes activities that promote the viability of the social and organizational network and enhance the psychological climate in which the technical core is embedded, activities such as helping and cooperating with others; following organizational rules and procedures even when personally inconvenient; endorsing, supporting, and defending organizational objectives; persisting with extra enthusiasm when necessary to complete own tasks successfully; and volunteering to carry out task activities that are not formally part of the job.

We should note that although the initial attempt to distinguish conceptually between contextual and task performance (Borman & Motowidlo, 1993) included motivational elements such as persisting and volunteering in the definition of contextual performance and did not include such motivational elements in the definition of task performance, recent evidence suggests it might be empirically difficult to divorce task performance from motivation, at least when task performance is assessed through supervisory ratings (Van Scotter & Motowidlo, 1996). Perhaps it even makes better sense conceptually to leave the motivational elements attached to both the task and contextual sides of the performance domain. In that case, motivation to perform one's own tasks effectively, shown in part through persistence and volunteering, would account for some of the variability in task performance; motivation to facilitate interpersonal, group, and organizational processes, support organizational objectives, and comply with rules and procedures, shown again in part through persistence and volunteering, would account for some of the variability in contextual performance. We introduce this possibility tentatively at this point and hope for more empirical work to settle the question of how motivational elements might be best handled in definitions of task and contextual performance.

The distinction between task and contextual behaviors boils down to two different explanations for a behavioral episode's contribution value for the organization. The reason task behaviors have positive contribution values is either that they help the transformation of raw materials into goods or services, or they directly service the organization's technical core and improve its capability to produce accordingly. The reason contextual behaviors have positive contribution values is that they maintain or improve the organizational, social, or psychological environment necessary for the technical core to function effectively and efficiently. In either case, the behaviors' contribution values represent their ultimate effects on organizational goal accomplishment, but through two quite different means.

INDIVIDUAL DIFFERENCES IN TASK AND CONTEXTUAL PERFORMANCE

Our theory focuses on individual difference variables as antecedents of task and contextual performance because we are concerned mostly with its implications for selection research in this article. Other kinds of determinants that might reflect the operation of motivation and training processes, for instance, are also interesting and important, but beyond the scope of this article. The theory borrows liberally from ideas developed by Hunter (1983); Campbell, McCloy, Oppler, and Sager (1993); McCrae and Costa (1996); and from a paper by Schmit, Motowidlo, DeGroot, Cross, and Kiker (1996) that attempted to explain mechanisms through which personality might affect job performance.

Hunter (1983) reported results of a meta-analysis of relations between measures of ability, job knowledge, work sample performance, and supervisory ratings of performance. Based on a total sample of 3,264 cases, he concluded that the causal model that fits the average correlations across all studies in his meta-analysis has direct causal paths from ability to both job knowledge and work sample performance, a direct path from job knowledge to work sample performance, and direct paths from both job knowledge and work sample performance to supervisory ratings of performance. Importantly, ability had no effect on supervisory ratings except through its effects on job knowledge and work sample performance. If work sample performance can be construed to be a measure of job skill (Campbell et al., 1996), and if supervisory ratings are, as we would argue, reasonable measures of job performance as defined by our model, Hunter's results show that ability directly affects job knowledge and skill and that it affects job performance only through its effects on knowledge and skill.

Campbell et al. (1993) and Campbell et al. (1996) presented a theory of performance that formalized relations Hunter showed between ability, job knowledge and skill, and job performance. They argued that there are three direct determinants of job performance: declarative knowledge, procedural knowledge and skill, and motivation. Declarative knowledge is knowledge of facts, principles, and procedures, knowledge that might be measured, for example, by the kinds of paper-and-pencil tests included in Hunter's meta-analysis. Procedural knowledge and skill is skill in actually doing what should be done. It is the combination of knowing what to do and actually being able to do it. It includes skills such as cognitive skill, psychomotor skill, physical skill, self-management skill, and interpersonal skill and might be measured by job sample tests like those included in Hunter's meta-analysis. Motivation is the combination of choice to exert effort, choice of how much effort to exert, and choice of how long to continue to exert effort. Individual differences in personality, ability, and interests are presumed to combine and interact with education, training, and experience to shape declarative knowledge and procedural knowledge and skill.

McCrae and Costa (1996) presented a metatheoretical framework that started from a very different intellectual tradition from that represented in work by Hunter (1983) and Campbell et al. (1993), but ended with remarkably similar implications for the pattern of relations between traits such as ability and personality, job knowledge and skill, and job performance. Their framework was designed to summarize the kinds of variables that all theories of personality, including the five-factor model, must be concerned with. It describes relations between five broad categories of variables—basic tendencies, characteristic adaptations, objective biography, self-concept, and external influences. Of these, the most relevant for our present purposes are basic tendencies, characteristic adaptations, and objective biography.

Basic tendencies are the fundamental capacities and dispositions that describe differences between individuals. They are abstractions that define potential for observable behavior. They can be inherited or shaped to some degree by early experience, but they are generally stable and enduring enough to give a consistent direction to people's lives. They include variables such as sensory-motor capacities, physical abilities, perceptual styles, learning ability, verbal ability, spatial ability, and personality traits such as the big five—extraversion, agreeableness, conscientiousness, neuroticism, and openness to experience.

Characteristic adaptations are the concrete expressions of abstract basic tendencies and take the form of specific skills, habits, preferences, attitudes, and patterns of behavior that people learn as their basic tendencies interact with their environments over time. Thus, characteristic adaptations are the joint product of basic tendencies and learning processes. They include variables such as general knowledge, language competencies, schemas and strategies, social skills, technical skills, religious attitudes, moral values, social and political attitudes, preferences, vocational interests, habits, daily routines, and social roles. Declarative knowledge and procedural knowledge and skill as defined by Campbell et al. (1993) are characteristic adaptations in this framework.

Objective biography is the set of overt behaviors that theories of personality often try to predict. In our terms, objective biography is job performance.

Causal relations between these three variables are particularly important for our purposes. The metatheoretical framework developed by McCrae and Costa (1996) presumes that basic tendencies directly affect characteristic adaptations that, in turn, directly affect objective biography. There is no direct link between basic tendencies and objective biography. The only causal connection between basic tendencies and objective biography is through characteristic adaptations.

These empirical and theoretical contributions by Hunter (1983), Campbell et al. (1993), and McCrae and Costa (1996) have in common the idea that effects of basic individual difference variables, such as ability and personality, on job performance are mediated by other variables. In Hunter's model, the mediating variables are knowledge and skill (work sample performance). In Campbell's et al. model, they are declarative knowledge, procedural knowledge and skill, and motivation. And in McCrae and Costa's model, they are characteristic adaptations that include variables such as knowledge and skill.

Our theory incorporates this idea. It maintains that individual differences in personality and cognitive ability, in combination with learning experiences, lead to variability in characteristic adaptations that mediate effects of personality and cognitive ability on job performance. An especially important aspect of this theory is that the kinds of traits and characteristic adaptations that are related to task performance are different from the kinds of traits and characteristic adaptations that are related to contextual performance. The theory is shown graphically in Figure 1.

The theory divides job performance into two groups of dimensions, task performance and contextual performance. It also includes two categories of basic tendencies: cognitive ability and personality. As mentioned, cognitive ability is presumed to be a better predictor of task performance and personality variables such as extraversion, agreeableness, and conscientiousness are presumed to be better predictors of contextual performance. Although the strongest effects of cognitive ability are on task performance, the theory predicts that cognitive ability also has some effect on contextual performance through its effects on characteristic adaptations that directly affect contextual performance. Similarly, although the strongest effects of personality variables are on contextual performance, the theory predicts that some personality variables also have some effect on task performance

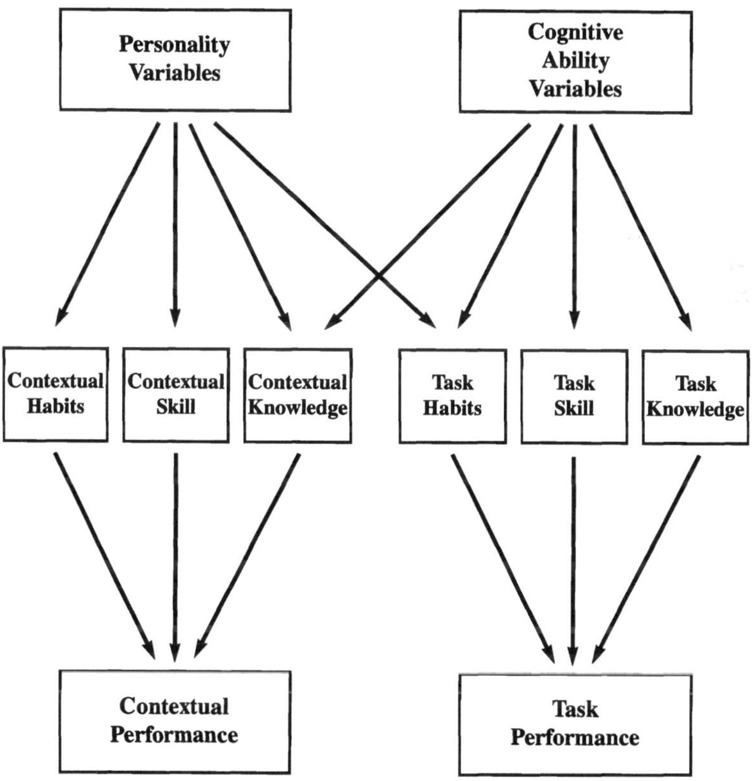

FIGURE 1 A theory of individual differences in task and contextual performance.

through their effects on aspects of characteristic adaptations that directly affect task performance. Despite these "crossover" effects, however, we still expect that personality is most strongly associated with the contextual side of the performance domain and that cognitive ability is most strongly associated with the task side of the performance domain.

The intervening variables in our theory are characteristic adaptations in knowledge, skills, and work habits. They are learned through experience as basic tendencies in ability and personality interact with external influences in the environment. One set of knowledge, skills, and habits directly affects task performance and another set directly affects contextual performance. Task knowledge, task skills, and task habits affect task performance by increasing the likelihood that people will perform behavioral episodes that have positive contribution values because they help an organization's technical core produce its goods and services. Contextual knowledge, contextual skills, and contextual habits affect contextual performance by increasing the likelihood that people will perform behavioral episodes that have positive contribution values because they promote the viability of the social and organizational network and enhance the psychological climate in which the technical core is embedded. Each of these mediating variables is described more fully in the paragraphs that follow.

Task knowledge is knowledge of facts and principles related to functions of the organization's technical core. It is also knowledge of procedures, judgmental heuristics, and rules for processing information and making decisions about matters related to the technical core. Task knowledge is shaped largely by cognitive ability; people with high levels of cognitive ability are more likely to master and remember relevant facts, principles, and procedures if they are provided with opportunities to learn them.

Contextual knowledge is knowledge of facts, principles, and procedures for effective action in situations that call for helping and cooperating with others; following organizational rules and procedures; endorsing, supporting, and defending organizational objectives; persisting despite difficult obstacles; and volunteering. Examples of contextual knowledge include knowing how to cooperate with a diverse group of people; knowing how to calm an upset worker; knowing how to work productively with difficult peers, supervisors, and subordinates; knowing how to present a favorable image of the organization to outsiders; knowing how to defend a supervisor's actions; and so forth. We expect that people whose personality characteristics are consistent with these elements of contextual knowledge should be more likely to notice that certain patterns of behavior are more effective in such situations and thus should be more likely to master this knowledge. For example, when actions that reflect high levels of extraversion or agreeableness are the most effective responses to difficult interpersonal and social challenges, people high on these traits should be more likely to learn this. But cognitive ability should also have some effect on the acquisition of contextual knowledge to the extent that information processing, memory processes, and decision making are important for determining that one kind of interpersonal or social response is more effective than another.

Task skill is skill in actually using technical information, performing technical procedures, handling information, making judgments, solving problems, and making decisions related to core technical functions. It involves skill in applying relevant technical knowledge to perform the necessary actions smoothly, quickly, and without error. As shown in Hunter's (1983) analysis of relations between cognitive ability, task skill (as assessed through work sample performance), and job performance (as assessed through supervisory ratings), cognitive ability has direct effects on task knowledge that, together with task skill, also mediates effects of ability on job performance.

Similarly, contextual skill is skill in actually carrying out actions known to be effective for handling situations that call for helping and coordinating with others; following organizational rules and procedures; endorsing, supporting, and defending organizational objectives; persisting; and volunteering. Contextual skills like these are determined largely by personality traits such as extraversion and agreeableness, and perhaps by other personality traits too that are consistent with the type of response required by challenging interpersonal and social situations.

Work habits are patterns of behavior that people learn over time and that can either facilitate or interfere with the performance of behaviors that contribute to the accomplishment of organizational goals. Like the other characteristic adaptations, they too are formed through the interaction of basic traits with environmental influences. They are stylistic ways of dealing with various classes of situations that occur on the job, but they are not necessarily the best or most effective ways of dealing with these situations. People might know what should be done in a particular work situation, and they might have the skill necessary to do it, but they might also have habitual responses to such situations that conflict with their tendencies to do what they know should be done.

Work habits include characteristic motivational responses such as easy shortcuts in task execution that people might take instead of going to the trouble to do the task as it should be done for maximum effectiveness; choices for how much effort to exert and for how long; tendencies to approach or avoid different kinds of situations in which they might have opportunities to contribute to organizational goals; procrastination; persistence in the face of setbacks and adversity; attention to detail; careful planning versus impulsivity; and so forth. They also include characteristic responses to situations that do not necessarily reflect motivational processes. For instance, sales representatives might know that the best way to deal with angry customers is to stay calm, empathize, and sincerely offer to find a solution, and they might be able to do this after training and practice. However, they might still find themselves occasionally reverting to old (pretraining) habits by feeling defensive and reacting with hostility in such situations, only to kick themselves later with the thought that they should have behaved differently.

Task work habits are patterns of responses to task situations that either facilitate or interfere with the performance of task behaviors. They include characteristic ways of using technical information, performing technical procedures, making decisions, and so on that may or may not be consistent with what the performers know are the most effective way to do these things. They also include motivational task habits such as characteristic tendencies to exert high or low levels of effort, focus sustained effort on a task, fall prey to distraction, and set challenging personal goals. We expect that task habits are affected by individual differences both in cognitive ability and in personality traits such as conscientiousness.

Contextual work habits are patterns of responses that either facilitate or interfere with effective performance in contextual work situations. They include characteristic tendencies to approach or avoid various types of interpersonal and group situations, preferred ways of handling conflict, interpersonal and political styles such as Machiavellianism, characteristic communication styles, and so forth. Like task work habits, they too might be at least somewhat affected by conscientiousness, but we expect that other personality traits that reflect tendencies to adopt one interpersonal or social style rather than another, traits such as extraversion and agreeableness, for instance, are more important determinants of these contextual habits.

SUMMARY

According to our theory of individual differences in task and contextual performance, the frequency and contribution value of behavioral episodes in the performance domain are determined directly by relevant knowledge, skills, and work habits. Behavioral episodes in the task part of the domain are determined by knowledge, skills, and habits that are different from those that affect behavioral episodes in the contextual part of the domain. Cognitive ability affects task performance through its effects on task knowledge, skills, and habits, and it may also affect contextual performance through its effects on contextual knowledge. Personality traits affect contextual performance through their effects on contextual knowledge, skills, and habits. One personality trait in particular, conscientiousness, may also affect task performance through its effects on task habits. In turn, task knowledge, task skills, and task habits directly account for individual differences in task performance whereas contextual knowledge, contextual skills, and contextual habits directly account for individual differences in contextual performance.

REFERENCES

Borman, W. C., & Motowidlo, S. J. (1993). Expanding the criterion domain to include elements of contextual performance. In N. Schmit & W. C. Borman (Eds.), *Personnel selection in organizations* (pp. 71–98). San Francisco: Jossey-Bass.

Campbell, J. P. (1983). Some possible implications of "modeling" for the conceptualization of measurement. In F. Landy, S. Zedeck, & J. Cleveland (Eds.), *Performance measurement and theory* (pp. 277–298). Hillsdale, NJ: Lawrence Erlbaum Associates, Inc.

Campbell, J. P. (1990). Modeling the performance prediction problem in industrial and organizational psychology. In M. D. Dunnette & L.M. Hough (Eds.), *Handbook of industrial and organizational psychology* (Vol. 1, 2nd ed.; pp. 687–732). Palo Alto, CA: Consulting Psychologists Press.

Campbell, J. P., Gasser, M. B., & Oswald, F. L. (1996). The substantive nature of job performance variability. In K. R. Murphy (Ed.), *Individual differences and behavior in organizations* (pp. 258–299). San Francisco: Jossey-Bass.

Campbell, J. P., McCloy, R. A., Oppler, S. H., & Sager, C. E. (1993). A theory of performance. In N. Schmit & W. C. Borman (Eds.), *Personnel selection in organizations* (pp. 35–70). San Francisco: Jossey-Bass.

Flanagan, J. C. (1954). The critical incident technique. *Psychological Bulletin, 51,* 327–358.

Hunter, J. E. (1983). A causal analysis of cognitive ability, job knowledge, job performance, and supervisor ratings. In F. Landy, S. Zedeck, & J. Cleveland (Eds.), *Performance measurement and theory* (pp. 257–266). Hillsdale, NJ: Lawrence Erlbaum Associates, Inc.

McCrae, R. R., & Costa, P. T. (1996). Toward a new generation of personality theories: Theoretical contexts for the five-factor model. In J. S. Wiggins (Ed.), *The five-factor model of personality* (pp. 51–87). New York: Guilford.

Motowidlo, S. J., Dunnette, M. D., & Carter, G. W. (1990). An alternative selection procedure: The low-fidelity simulation. *Journal of Applied Psychology, 75,* 640–647.

Motowidlo, S. J., & Van Scotter, J. R. (1994). Evidence that task performance should be distinguished from contextual performance. *Journal of Applied Psychology, 79,* 475–480.

Newtson, D. (1973). Attribution and the unit of perception of ongoing behavior. *Journal of Personality and Social Psychology, 28,* 28–38.

Newtson, D., Engquist, G., & Bois, J. (1977). The objective basis of behavior units. *Journal of Personality and Social Psychology, 35,* 847–862.

Schmit, M. C., Motowidlo, S. J., DeGroot, T., Cross, T., & Kiker, D. S. (1996, April). *Explaining the relationship between personality and job performance.* Paper presented at the meeting of the Society for Industrial and Organizational Psychology, San Diego, CA.

Van Scotter, J. R., & Motowidlo, S. J. (1996). Interpersonal facilitation and job dedication as separate facets of contextual performance. *Journal of Applied Psychology, 81,* 525–531.

HUMAN PERFORMANCE, *10*(2), 85–97

Organizational Citizenship Behavior: It's Construct Clean-Up Time

Dennis W. Organ
School of Business
Indiana University

Accumulated empirical evidence, some telling criticisms, and even the most cursory glance at the business press compel us to rethink the defining character of organizational citizenship behavior (OCB). It no longer seems fruitful to regard OCB as "extra-role," "beyond the job," or "unrewarded by the formal system." A more tenable position is one that defines OCB much along the lines of what Borman and Motowidlo (1993) called *contextual performance.* Some preliminary suggestions are offered for the repositioning and articulation of the OCB construct as redefined; due attention is given to the problems that nonetheless remain, and will occupy us for some time to come as we reckon with root changes in the very character of organizations.

In concluding my account of the "good soldier syndrome" (Organ, 1988), I freely admitted to some "discomfiting softness" in a "working definition" of organizational citizenship behavior (OCB). I made this admission in a chapter titled "Unfinished Business." Perhaps the business of conceptual refinement is never finished, but it is high time to revisit some questions pertaining to construct definitions, terminology, and basic models.

Already one substantial review of construct definitions and nomological networks related to OCB has appeared (Van Dyne, Cummings, & Parks, 1995). As will soon become clear, I find much to appreciate in that discussion. However, I differ with them on some important issues and I raise some other issues that they chose not to address.

Van Dyne et al. (1995) addressed the following issues: (a) the muddled state of overlap among several constructs of extra-role behavior (ERB): OCB, prosocial organizational behavior (POB), principled organizational dissent (POD), and whistle-blowing (WB); (b) the case for the utility of the larger construct, ERB; and (c)

Requests for reprints should be sent to Dennis W. Organ, School of Business, Indiana University, Bloomington, IN 47405. E-mail: organ@indiana.edu the plausible sets of antecedents and consequences of redefined categories of ERB. Along the way, Van Dyne et al. argued for making do without the construct POB because of its excessive breadth, a position already concurred with by the two coauthors of that term. Curiously though, Van Dyne et al. took no account of two other constructs—organizational spontaneity (OS; George & Brief, 1992) and contextual performance (Borman & Motowidlo, 1993; Motowidlo & Van Scotter, 1994). Brief and Motowidlo (1986) first presented the idea of POB, but left it behind in search of more precise notions.

My agenda here is more limited. I wish to look at the persistent problems that astute people (including myself) have observed with respect to the working definition of OCB and offer some suggestions toward ameliorating those problems. Of necessity, a considerable amount of empirical research is reviewed, because the data from that research make important statements about the viability of one or another positions with regard to definitions, taxonomies, and nomological nets. But in the main, the discussion here is not about hypotheses to be researched or the documentation of substantive relations or even methodology in the usual sense. What is hoped for is simply a way of thinking about OCB that we can be comfortable with.

THE WORKING DEFINITION

My 1988 monograph defined OCB as "individual behavior that is discretionary, not directly or explicitly recognized by the formal reward system, and that in the aggregate promotes the effective functioning of the organization" (Organ, 1988, p. 4).

That definition, with very minor stylistic differences, preserved the one offered earlier in Bateman and Organ (1983) and Smith, Organ, and Near (1983); an updated account (Organ, 1990) retained it as well. Anticipating some of the criticisms that came later, I immediately elaborated on and qualified the three "soft spots" in that definition:

> By *discretionary,* we mean that the behavior is not an *enforceable* [italics added] requirement of the role or the job description, that is the clearly specifiable terms of the person's employment contract with the organization; the behavior is rather a matter of personal choice, such that its omission is not generally understood as punishable. (Organ, 1988, p. 4)

(Note that even the qualifiers are qualified, e.g., pointed use of the adverbs "clearly," and "generally." Thus, the discipline of academic writing makes cowards of us all, such that we are loath to say anything that is not qualified.)

I went on to add:

> Our definition of OCB requires that it not be *directly* or *formally* recompensed by the organization's reward system. ... [Does this] mean that OCB must be limited to those

> gestures that are utterly and eternally lacking in any tangible return to the individual? ... Not necessarily. Over time, a steady stream of OCB of different types ... could well determine the impression that an individual makes on a supervisor or on coworkers. That impression, in turn, could influence the recommendation by the boss for a salary increase or promotion. The important issue here is that such returns not be contractually guaranteed. (Organ, 1988, p. 5)

In other words, I was thinking of OCB as contributions that might—or might not—invite some future recompense. The point is that the rewards that accrue to OCB are at best indirect and uncertain, as compared to more formal contributions such as high productivity or technical excellence or innovative solutions. Those contributions would have a greater likelihood of being expressly linked to the formal reward system.

Finally, it was required that OCB contain only those behaviors that, in the aggregate, across time and across persons, contribute to organizational effectiveness. In other words, not every single discrete instance of OCB would make a difference in organizational outcomes; for example, I might offer help to a coworker that actually turns out to be dysfunctional for that person's performance, but summated across the categories of relevant behaviors, the effect would be positive. Or, if you will, lots of people who frequently offer help to coworkers will contribute to the effectiveness of their organization.

This latter requirement as a definition of OCB was one that I thought would ultimately have to be an exercise in faith. The concept of *organizational effectiveness,* its operational definition, and its temporal relation to any of its many antecedents, all loomed as formidable and perhaps impossible conditions to demonstrate. As it happens, though, several studies have taken on the forbidding task of testing the relation between OCB and effectiveness, and the results—while hardly conclusive, because they are cross-sectional—are consistently supportive (Karambaya, 1991; Podsakoff, Ahearne, & MacKenzie, in press; Podsakoff & MacKenzie, 1994; Walz & Niehoff, 1996).

The discretionary and noncontractual reward requirements of the definition have elicited much more discussion and criticism of the OCB construct, as well as its usual forms of measurement. And the problems noted with respect to this demand a reconsideration of the utility of these defining requirements; as we will see, they might still figure as descriptive attributes that, in a probabilistic sense, differentiate OCB from other constructs.

Problems With "Discretionary"

In brief, the problem noted with OCB defined as discretionary, extra-role, and beyond the job requirements is that OCB, as measured, contains elements that many observers (even the respondents themselves) would consider part of the job. Thus, Morrison (1994) reported that 18 of 20 OCB items were described by a majority of respondents as "in-role." Moreover, participants in her study differed in their conception of the "breadth" of the job. Morrison concluded that "OCB is ill-defined and varies from one employee to the next and between employees and supervisors" (Morrison, 1994, p. 1561). One could interpret this as more of a measurement issue rather than a construct problem, but often the two turn out to be very much intertwined. Construct clarity is not a sufficient condition for psychometric soundness, but it probably is a necessary condition.

Perhaps the problem with defining OCB as extra-role or beyond the job requirements inheres in the very fuzziness of the concepts "role" and "job" themselves. As the work of Graen and others on leader-member exchange (Dansereau, Graen, & Haga, 1975; Graen & Uhl-Bien, 1995) has long documented, roles evolve from leader–subordinate give-and-take. Katz and Kahn (1966), in articulating their open-systems model of organizations, explicitly defined roles in terms of the expectations of "role senders," and obviously "expectations" can vary from expecting something well beneath any formal job requirements to something far beyond them. It seems that we guarantee construct muddiness if we define OCB as requiring that it be extra-role.

Van Dyne et al. (1995) vigorously defended the viability of ERB as a construct. They freely conceded that observers will differ across persons and times as to what is exactly in-role or extra-role, and therefore it is somewhat arbitrary in many instances as to what is actually extra-role. However, arguing forcefully with an analogy to the arbitrariness of what we choose to call "green" or "blue" or "aqua," which certainly does not render the concept of "green" (or the concept of "color") valueless, Van Dyne et al. insisted that ERB and in-role behavior (IRB) are useful theoretical building blocks. Thus, one would infer that their position regards any problem here as pertaining more to measurement than construct definition.

My own position is that it would be preferable to avoid, if we could, reference to ERB in defining OCB. As noted earlier, roles evolve as a function of expectations and role-sending; somehow it seems odd that what would be considered OCB today would be regarded as something else next month, or that what a supervisor thinks is OCB is assessed as IRB by some peers or subordinates. I do not see the Van Dyne et al. (1995) position as untenable, but I would want to exhaust other possibilities first.

What about extra-job? I think most students of these matters would concede a distinction between role and job, particularly if by job we mean some sort of formal job description. Thinking this way leaves us pretty much where we started in 1988, that is, OCB is discretionary in the sense of going beyond the enforceable requirement of the job description.

My response to this proposal is that there are probably rampant ambiguities regarding what enforceable job requirements consist of. Jobs, like roles, are changing, in the wake of downsizing, flattening, team-based, flexform organizations. Indeed, a cover story of *Fortune* magazine titled "The End of the Job" (1994) suggested that the "job" is a social artifact and no longer the best way to organize work. If what they are saying has any empirical foundation whatsoever, then one suspects that such formal job descriptions as are still being written are couched in increasing levels of abstractions and generalities. The job will be whatever is required in the person's workplace, contingent on the necessary training having been provided. To the extent this occurs, OCB would have been defined away, because anything that is needed from the person in order to contribute would have been part of the job.

The Problem With Noncontractual Rewards

If neither role nor job provide a convenient point of departure for defining OCB, what about the rewards issue? The working definition, we need to remember, did not rule out some sort of reward consequence for a behavior to qualify as OCB, only that it not be contractually guaranteed by the formal reward system. The problem with this is that very few rewards are contractually guaranteed for any behavior, including technical performance or brilliant innovation. How many professors can say they are "guaranteed" promotion, tenure, or an above-average salary increase, regardless of how much or how well they publish, or how good their student evaluations are? In the downsizing of the 1980s and 1990s, how many people employed in private business can even guarantee their continued employment, regardless of how consistently well they have performed? How many top management people would even gingerly guarantee any employee benefit anymore—having learned that even the IBMs of the world can be blind-sided by competition?

Indeed, to the extent that "rewards" follow from appraisals of performance, research (MacKenzie, Podsakoff, & Fetter, 1991; Podsakoff & MacKenzie, 1994; Werner, 1994) now strongly suggests that some forms of OCB might be just as likely as—if not more likely than—in-role performance to lead to monetary recompense. Orr, Sackett, and Mercer (1989) reported that managers have no reluctance to put a dollar value on most of the behaviors that we have been calling OCB.

So, where do we stand? Of the three essential conditions for OCB, we are left with one—that it contribute to organizational effectiveness. If that is all we have, then we might as well call it "performance" or "contribution" and be done with it.

OCB AS CONTEXTUAL PERFORMANCE

As noted previously, Van Dyne et al.'s (1995) discussion made no reference to Borman and Motowidlo's contextual performance (Borman & Motowidlo, 1993;

Motowidlo & Van Scotter, 1994). Because Borman and Motowidlo (1993) defined this as "behaviors [that] do not support the technical core itself so much as they support the broader organizational, social, and psychological environment in which the technical core must function" (p. 73), there is clearly overlap here with such notions as OCB and ERB.

Borman and Motowidlo (1993) enumerated five categories of contextual performance, including volunteering for activities beyond a person's formal job expectations, persistence of enthusiasm and application when needed to complete important task requirements, assistance to others, following rules and prescribed procedures even when it is inconvenient, and openly espousing and defending organization objectives. Obviously, the enumerated categories sound much like OCB in the form of altruism, compliance, sportsmanship, courtesy, and civic virtue (at least as the latter has been operationalized in studies of OCB dimensions). What is different from OCB is that contextual performance as defined does not require that the behavior be extra-role nor that it be nonrewarded. The defining quality is that it be "non-task," or more to the point, that it contribute to the maintenance and/or enhancement of the context of work. Some such contributions might well lie within the explicit expectations of what constitutes appropriate role behavior and some could well earn emoluments from the formal reward system via the effect on performance appraisals.

Some readers might object to defining OCB as Borman and Motowidlo define contextual performance, regarding it as too vague or diffuse. And indeed, it could be that we have just introduced still more concepts that cry out for clarity. What do we mean by "social and psychological environment"? What do we mean by "support" in reference to such environments? A good initial test of any construct, say *X,* is to see if we can designate some things that certainly are not *X.* I am hard pressed to think of many nontrivial actions that would most certainly not, in one way or another, "support the social and psychological environment."

On balance, though, I am inclined to counter this objection to diffuseness by saying that it is premature and should await tests of our ability to develop measures that demonstrate convergent and, especially, discriminant validity. In fact, Motowidlo and Van Scotter (1994) already empirically demonstrated, in a study of 421 Air Force mechanics, that measures of task performance and contextual performance have different predictors, and more to the point, that they contribute independently to ratings of overall performance. Contextual performance is, to be sure, couched at a rather high level of abstraction. But if that continues to bother us, it is a condition that can be remedied by some mix of conceptual and empirical work that provides molar or "mid range" constructs, that is, classes of contextual performance. These might or might not bear much resemblance to the categories of altruism, compliance, sportsmanship, courtesy, and the like.

Another consideration in favor of the task/contextual dichotomy is the long tradition in group and organizational studies of similar distinctions. One thinks, for example, of Bales' pioneering lab studies of small groups, in which he saw roles of task and maintenance specialists emerge (Bales & Slater, 1955); of Fleishman's field studies of leadership, finding that initiating structure and consideration were independent dimensions of formal leader behavior (Fleishman, Harris, & Burtt, 1955); of Katz and Kahn's (1966) distinction between production systems and maintenance, political, and adaptive systems. Even the Hawthorne studies (Roethlisberger & Dickson, 1939/1967), with the recognition of formal and informal leadership, and the sociological theory of Parsons (1960), distinguishing between the technical and institutional social systems, echo this duality.

My objection to contextual performance is not its definition but its name. It simply strikes me as cold, gray, and bloodless. Perhaps our formal constructs should be like that. For the moment, though, I would like to hold on to OCB, at the very least for certain milieus of discourse, because I find that both academic and practitioner types readily and intuitively grasp what it is all about. They might quibble over both the existing and any newly proffered definitions, but in the larger sense they see the point. Perhaps the research community will settle on yet a different moniker for its own internal purposes, but even so I think the tag OCB would come in handy as we disseminate our insights and findings to broader constituencies.

THE NOMOLOGICAL NET

So, if we redefine OCB as contributions to the maintenance and enhancement of the social and psychological context that supports task performance (or the technical/technological/production system?), how do we construe the larger nomological net that identifies and enriches such a construct?

First, I would suggest that, compared to task performance, OCB (now conceived as synonymous with contextual performance) is less likely to be considered an enforceable job requirement, to the extent that such requirements continue to exist in organizations. Second, I would suggest that OCB in its revised definition is less likely than task performance to be regarded by the performer as leading confidently to systemic rewards. Although research has demonstrated that exceptional display of OCB can influence performance evaluations and that managers are willing to put a dollar value on some forms of OCB, it is doubtful that the persons rendering these contributions would see a one-to-one correspondence between discrete instances of such contributions and near-term payoffs. The major exception to this statement would obviously be those jobs that, by their nature, virtually consist of varied forms of contextual performance. Counselors, ombudsmen, and some human resource staff functions might fit this exception.

The exceptions, even if they turn out to be numerous, still constitute inordinate construct problems, because now we do not require as a construct definition that

OCB be "beyond the job" or "not lead to system rewards." We are, rather, offering an empirical testable hypothesis to the effect that performance contributions in the two forms—OCB and task—differ by degree in the matters of enforceable job requirements and guarantee of systemic rewards.

Thirdly, as indicated earlier, I find much to agree with in Van Dyne et al.'s (1995) discussion, excepting their positive regard for the in-role/extra-role distinction. I would, for example, second their motion that we regard OCB as "affiliative" and "promotive." I agree with them that construct clarity is aided by preserving the distinction between OCB and "challenging" behaviors (such as POD or WB), which have a different character altogether: Although there is no gainsaying that such challenges can and sometimes do ultimately contribute to an organization's survival and long-run effectiveness, they do so at the risk of severe short-term costs to the social and psychological context that supports task performance. Put differently, challenging behaviors—however appropriate and needed they might be—often pit brother against brother, sister against sister, ins against outs, haves against have-nots, and so forth. Challenges present shocks to the system. Sometimes these shocks are needed, but they do present risks.

Early on, I noted in Graham's "civic virtue," or responsible involvement in the governance and political system of an organization (Graham, 1986), an important form of contribution "beyond what is required by the formal system," and thus something that ought to be subsumed under OCB. However, anyone familiar with the research on OCB knows how civic virtue was garbled in the process of operationalization—it came out in questionnaire rating items that referred to attending meetings, keeping up with what was going on, reading and responding to announcements and mail. Something go lost in the process, and here's why.

Origins of OCB

The roots of OCB research and theory lie in an intuitive conviction that, contrary to the then-in-vogue party line of industrial/organizational psychology, job satisfaction did indeed bear a functional relation to performance of a sort (Organ, 1977). Although granting that job attitudes might have little to do with objective measures of individual job output, the argument was that satisfaction would affect people's willingness to help colleagues and work associates and their disposition to cooperate in varied and mundane forms to maintain organized structures that govern work. Putting the argument in these terms meant that there was scant interest in looking at such things as POD. We do not generally think of people who "challenge," or criticize, the established order as people who are most satisfied with it.

The need to identify more precisely those helpful and cooperative behaviors borne of job satisfaction led Smith (Smith et al., 1983) to visit several lower-level managers at their places of work. Using a tape recorder, Smith simply asked these people:

> What kinds of things do you like to have people in your group do, but you know that you can't actually force them to do it, can't promise any tangible rewards for doing it, and can't punish them for not doing it?

Smith got the richly textured material that she sought and went on from there to develop the instrument that has been the most widely used in research on OCB. But deriving the instrument this way ensured a "managerial" or, if you wish, "status quo," bias to the measure and thus, in effect, to any honest interpretation of the research using that measure. In other words, OCB became, operationally, "things that supervisors like for you to do, even though they can't make you do it and can't guarantee any reward for it beyond their appreciation and perhaps an occasional extra kindness or two." Moreover, one could have bet that the behaviors identified would tend toward the mundane—rather than, say, bold innovative suggestions. One suspects that most managers are trying to minimize present headaches, not trying to multiply them by entertaining scores of initiatives from their charges.

But, in retrospect, perhaps the unintentioned bias toward what kind of performance results from satisfaction and what managers appreciate is not unfortunate, at least from a theoretical perspective. What was unfortunate was not making it explicit. Worse yet, trying to subsume too much under the construct, and then operationalizing ill-fitting molar constructs (such as civic virtue) into the same kind of items found in the early OCB measure, occasioned confusion. Recognizing that to be the case now, we can proceed explicitly with what we started out with, but now with much more well-defined boundaries. To regard OCB as affiliative and promotive, as suggested by Van Dyne et al. (1995), has much to recommend it.

Antecedents

I have a quibble, though, with Van Dyne et al.'s (1995) description of OCB antecedents as *affective states.* The quibble arises because, of late, some readers would equate affective states with mood states. Readers do so because some writers have chosen to define mood as affective state (e.g., George & Brief, 1992, and various social psychological works from which they draw). However, affect and affective have been used in psychological discourse in ways that do not necessarily say anything about mood. The conventional psychological definition of an attitude, for example, refers to an affective component or "the intensity of positive or negative affect for or against a psychological object" (Worchel, Cooper, & Goethals, 1988, p. 200). This does not mean that people with positive attitudes toward their employers are necessarily in a "good mood" at any particular time. It simply means that the cognitions clustered in association with the employer contain positive evaluations or assessments.

Furthermore, in a recent meta-analysis of attitudinal and dispositional correlates of OCB (Organ & Ryan, 1995), little support was found for the ability of mood-state or mood-trait measures to predict OCB. Rather, it was found that affectively toned descriptions of the organization and its leadership—to wit, job satisfaction, perceived fairness, leader supportiveness, and organizational commitment—predicted both Altruism and Compliance at about the same level. It would appear that it is what such measures have in common, as attitudes, that really relates to OCB. And we might do well simply to refer to that common ground as something akin to the old-fashioned notion of "morale."

The meta-analytic review also found next to nothing in the way of dispositional predictors of OCB; the sole exception was that various measures that appear to overlap around a core concept of "conscientiousness" are modestly associated with Compliance, or the more impersonal variety of OCB.

Thus, if I had to offer up a statement of antecedents of OCB, I would prefer a more parsimonious version than that proposed by Van Dyne et al. (1995). In place of the six affective states, I think it is more appropriate to put "attitudes indicative of or derived from a general state of morale in the workplace." Instead of their six individual differences dimensions, we might do well just to refer to "dispositions related to conscientiousness" and "any dispositions that can be confidently and empirically tied to characteristic level of morale in the workplace."

DIMENSIONS OF OCB

One of the recurring objections to OCB terminology has been the use of the term *altruism* to denote those contributions to effectiveness that take the form of assistance to specific persons, such as colleagues, associates, clients, or the boss. The objection rests on the argument that to describe any such behavior as altruism is to impute a particular motive for the behavior, or at the least to imply that some motive devoid of self-interest is at work.

The point is well taken. We can do rather well by calling this form of OCB simply helping or helpfulness. If we really need something neutral and more likely to guard against preconceived connotations, we could follow the lead of Williams and Anderson (1991) and designate it as *OCB–I*—to indicate that the exemplars of this class of OCB contributions are those targeted toward an individual as they are acted out. Furthermore, we might well use this nomenclature also to refer to what has otherwise been separated out as *Courtesy,* those OCB gestures that are demonstrated in the interest of preventing problems that would otherwise occur for specifiable individuals. Empirical research has sometimes been able to sustain the distinction between what was termed Altruism and Courtesy, but not with consistent loading of the intended items on the factors.

Continuing with the Williams and Anderson labels, we can designate a dimension of OCB as that which offers no immediate aid to any specific person or persons, but demonstrates and sustains high standards for attendance, punctuality, conservation of organizational resources, and use of time while at work—and label it as *OCB–O,* to indicate that the organization or unit as an entity is the target. In time, perhaps someone will offer a useful tag, analogous to helping for OCB–I, that will capture the gist of this concept. I still am partial to the label *conscientiousness,* except that it invites confusion with a dimension of the Big Five group of personality factors. Perhaps that confusion is a tolerable, even trivial risk. After all, we use achievement motivation and anxiety as both state-descriptors and trait-descriptors.

THE "UNFINISHED BUSINESS" BEFORE US NOW

If we can assume some reasonable degree of consensus on the positions described here, then how do we now proceed? What are the problem areas?

No doubt the most formidable exercise awaiting us is develop a more precise rendering of what we mean when we define OCB as "performance that supports the social and psychological environment in which task performance takes place." Although that is a good place from which to start, we can scarcely be comfortable in leaving it at that. What we seem to be groping for is something that is in the essence of the very condition of social organization itself. This might be an issue whose treatment calls for some consultation with our "macro" colleagues in organization theory. Unfortunately, their literature is one that I cannot claim to have followed closely in recent years. But those readers who toil in the interstices of macro- and micro-organizational behavior might know of fruitful linkages that would help explicate a compelling description of the construct.

Such linkages might well aid us in yet another area of concern, which is the level of analysis problem. To date, most OCB and related research has addressed contributions by individuals and the antecedents of those contributions. A few studies have looked at the group or organizational level, but virtually entirely so in a straightforward aggregative and descriptive style. We are left with a "black box" of "process" (as is all too common in a discipline whose bread-and-butter methodology is the correlational field study). Although we have some reassuring data in support of the connection between OCB and systemic performance, little if any analysis has dealt with the means by which OCB has these effects. What is the chemistry by which the state of organization is altered by individual OCB? What sequences of stages are effected? What is the "half-life" of these stages and their effects?

CONCLUSION

The changes that are occurring in the workplace—changes that we already have written and talked about so often that their description has become a quilt of cliches—will no doubt cause us to reexamine many of our favored constructs in organizational psychology. Or at least that will be the case for the "organizational" part of our field, and that is the part that provides our raison d'etre. Although it does not seem to me that 1983 is exactly lost in the shrouded mist of history, it does appear now that the way I described OCB in that year was mightily influenced by fading attributes of a different kind of organization from the one we see taking shape now. One hopes that the refinements along the lines suggested here and by others will help to preserve whatever the idea of OCB had to offer.

REFERENCES

Bales, R. F., & Slater, P. (1955). Role differentiation in small decision-making groups. In T. Parsons & R. F. Bales (Eds.), *Family, socialization and interaction processes* (pp. 259–306). Glencoe, IL: Free Press.

Bateman, T. S., & Organ, D. W. (1983). Job satisfaction and the good soldier: The relationship between affect and employee "citizenship." *Academy of Management Journal, 26,* 587–595.

Borman, W. C., & Motowidlo, S. J. (1993). Expanding the criterion domain to include elements of contextual performance. In N. Schmitt & W. C. Borman (Eds.), *Personality selection* (pp. 71–98). San Francisco: Jossey-Bass.

Brief, A. P., & Motowidlo, S. J. (1986). Prosocial organizational behaviors. *Academy of Management Review, 10,* 710–725.

Dansereau, F. D., Jr., Graen, G., & Haga, W. J. (1975). A vertical dyad linkage approach to leadership within formal organizations: A longitudinal investigation of the role making process. *Organizational Behavior and Human Performance, 13,* 46–78.

The end of the job. (1994, September 19). *Fortune,* 62ff.

Fleishman, E. A., Harris, E. H., & Burtt, H. E. (1955). Leadership and supervision in industry. *Ohio State Business Educational Research Monograph* (No. 33). Columbus: The Ohio State University.

George, J. M., & Brief, A. P. (1992). Feeling good–doing good: A conceptual analysis of the mood at work-organizational spontaneity relationship. *Psychological Bulletin, 112,* 310–329.

Graen, G. B., & Uhl-Bien, M. (1995). Relationship-based approach to leadership: Development of leader-member exchange (LMX) theory of leadership over 25 years: Applying a multi-level multi-domain perspective. *Leadership Quarterly, 6,* 219–247.

Graham, J. W. (1986, August). *Organizational citizenship informed by political theory.* Paper presented at the meetings of the Academy of Management, Chicago.

Karambaya, R. (1991). *Contexts for organizational citizenship: Do high performing and satisfying units have better citizens?* Unpublished manuscript, York University, Ontario, Canada.

Katz, D., & Kahn, R. L. (1966). *The social psychology of organizations.* New York: Wiley.

MacKenzie, S. B., Podsakoff, P. M., & Fetter, R. (1991). Organizational citizenship behavior and objective productivity as determinants of managerial evaluations of salespersons' performance. *Organizational Behavior and Human Decision Processes, 50,* 123–150.

Morrison, E. W. (1994). Role definitions and organizational citizenship behavior: The importance of the employee's perspective. *Academy of Management Journal, 37,* 1543–1567.

Motowidlo, S. J., & Van Scotter, J. R. (1994). Evidence that task performance should be distinguished from contextual performance. *Journal of Applied Psychology, 79,* 475–480.

Organ, D. W. (1977). A reappraisal and reinterpretation of the satisfaction–causes–performance hypothesis. *Academy of Management Review, 2,* 46–53.

Organ, D. W. (1988). *Organizational citizenship behavior: The good soldier syndrome*. Lexington, MA: Lexington.

Organ, D. W. (1990). The motivational basis of organizational citizenship behavior. In B. M. Staw & L. L. Cummings (Eds.), *Research in organizational behavior: Vol. 12* (pp. 43–72). Greenwich, CT: JAI.

Organ, D. W., & Ryan, K. (1995). A meta-analytic review of attitudinal and dispositional predictors of organizational citizenship behavior. *Personnel Psychology, 48,* 775–800.

Orr, J. M., Sackett, P. R., & Mercer, M. (1989). The role of prescribed and nonprescribed behavior in estimating the dollar value of performance. *Journal of Applied Psychology, 74,* 34–40.

Parsons, T. (1960). *Structure and process in modern societies*. New York: Free Press.

Podsakoff, P. M., Ahearne, M., & MacKenzie, S. B. (in press). Organizational citizenship behavior and the quantity and quality of work group performance. *Journal of Applied Psychology.*

Podsakoff, P. M., & MacKenzie, S. B. (1994). Organizational citizenship behaviors and sales unit effectiveness. *Journal of Marketing Research, 31,* 351–363.

Roethlisberger, F. J., & Dickson, W. J. (1967). *Management and the worker*. Cambridge, MA: Harvard University Press. (Original work published 1939)

Smith, C. A., Organ, D. W., & Near, J. P. (1983). Organizational citizenship behavior: Its nature and antecedents. *Journal of Applied Psychology, 68,* 653–663.

Van Dyne, L., Cummings, L. L., & Parks, J. M. (1995). Extra role behaviors: In pursuit of construct and definitional clarity (a bridge over muddied waters). In L. L. Cummings & B. M. Staw (Eds.), *Research in organizational behavior* (Vol. 17, pp. 215–285). Greenwich, CT: JAI.

Walz, S. M., & Niehoff, B. P. (1996, August). *Organizational citizenship behaviors and their effect on organizational effectiveness in limited-menu restaurants.* Paper presented at the meetings of the Academy of Management, Cincinnati, OH.

Werner, J. M. (1994). Dimensions that make a difference: Examining the impact of in-role and extra-role behaviors on supervisory ratings. *Journal of Applied Psychology, 79,* 98–107.

Williams, L. J., & Anderson, S. E. (1991). Job satisfaction and organizational commitment as predictors of organizational citizenship and in-role behavior. *Journal of Management, 17,* 601–617.

Worchel, S., Cooper, J., & Goethals, G. R. (1988). *Understanding social psychology*. Chicago: Dorsey.

HUMAN PERFORMANCE, *10*(2), 99–109

Task Performance and Contextual Performance: The Meaning for Personnel Selection Research

Walter C. Borman
University of South Florida
Personnel Decisions Research Institutes

Stephan J. Motowidlo
Human Resource Research Center
University of Florida

This article distinguishes between task and contextual activities, and a taxonomy of contextual performance containing elements of organizational citizenship behavior and prosocial organizational behavior is offered. Evidence is presented demonstrating that supervisors weight roughly equally subordinate task and contextual performance when making overall judgments of their performance. This, along with data showing that personality successfully predicts contextual performance, provides an alternative explanation for recent meta-analytic findings that personality correlates moderately with overall performance. Personality may be predicting the contextual component of overall performance. Results from studies using the Hogan Personality Inventory confirm that correlations between personality and contextual criteria are higher than correlations between personality and overall performance. We argue that finding such links between predictors and individual criterion elements significantly advances the science of personnel selection.

Task performance can be defined as the effectiveness with which job incumbents perform activities that contribute to the organization's technical core either directly by implementing a part of its technological process, or indirectly by providing it with needed materials or services (Borman & Motowidlo, 1993). Examples of task

Requests for reprints should be sent to Walter C. Borman, Department of Psychology, BEH 339, University of South Florida, Tampa, FL 33620–8200.

performance dimensions for a sales job might include Product Knowledge, Closing the Sale, and Organization and Time Management. For a firefighter job, Performing Rescue Operations, Conducting Salvage Operations, and Applying Ventilation Procedures are good examples of task dimensions.

We have argued that contextual performance is different (Borman & Motowidlo, 1993). Contextual activities are important because they contribute to organizational effectiveness in ways that shape the organizational, social, and psychological context that serves as the catalyst for task activities and processes. Contextual activities include volunteering to carry out task activities that are not formally part of the job and helping and cooperating with others in the organization to get tasks accomplished. This article focuses on this distinction between task performance and contextual performance (Borman & Motowidlo, 1993) and discusses the impact of this distinction on personnel selection research.

Our taxonomy of contextual performance, presented next, borrows heavily from three previous concepts. First, Smith, Organ, and Near (1983) and Bateman and Organ (1983) introduced the notion of *organizational citizenship behavior* (OCB). These authors also pointed out that OCB itself draws significantly from earlier writings by Barnard (1938), Katz (1964), and Katz and Kahn (1978). OCB is defined as extra-role discretionary behavior intended to help others in the organization or to demonstrate conscientiousness in support of the organization. Regarding measurement of OCB, Smith et al. developed a 16-item survey that can be used as a self-report instrument or as rating scales for supervisors or peers to use in making OCB ratings. Generally, two factors emerge from factor analyses of correlations between item responses: (a) *Altruism,* or helping others, and (b) *Generalized Compliance,* following the rules and procedures of the organization (Organ, 1988).

Brief and Motowidlo (1986) discussed a very similar concept. They defined *prosocial organizational behavior* (POB) as behavior performed with the intention of promoting the welfare of individuals or groups to whom that behavior is directed. The major differences between OCB and POB are that POB can be either role-prescribed or extra-role, whereas OCB by definition is extra-role (Organ, 1988), and that POB can be negative for the organization but positive toward individuals. An example of the latter is helping a coworker with a personal problem and, because of that prosocial act, failing to meet an important deadline.

Finally, the model of soldier effectiveness comes from work done to identify performance constructs relevant to first-tour soldiers that are important for unit effectiveness but that fall outside technical proficiency kinds of performance requirements (Borman, Motowidlo, Rose, & Hanser, 1985). The conceptual model, shown in Figure 1, argues that the concepts of organizational socialization, organizational commitment, and morale essentially combine to define three major performance dimensions. Commitment and socialization merge to define Allegiance; socialization and morale come together to define Teamwork; and morale

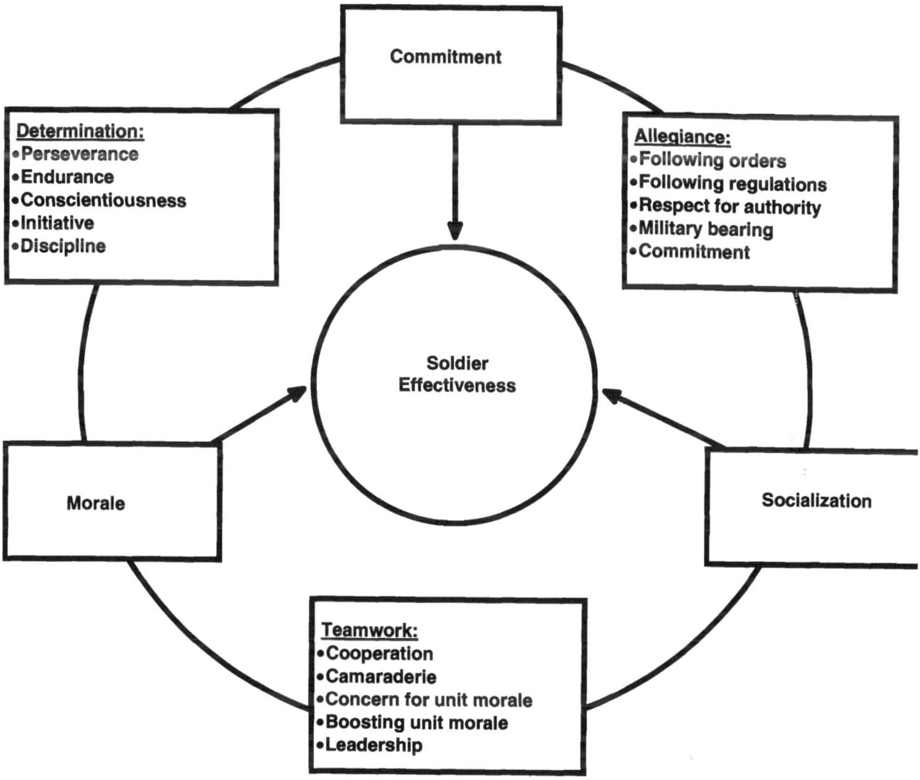

FIGURE 1 Soldier effectiveness model.

and commitment combine to yield Determination. Then each of these dimensions decomposes into five subdimensions as depicted in the model.

Other related concepts are also considered in our taxonomy of contextual performance. Organ (1988) discussed *Sportsmanship* or a "lack of complaining"—it is sometimes observed in management literature that 10% of employees take up 90% of a supervisor's time. Our observation is that this is a complex dimension with respect to its relation with some aspects of organizational effectiveness and societal well-being. *Whistleblowing* might be viewed as defining the lowest point on this dimension, and yet these acts have often been quite "morally effective" (e.g., Near & Miceli, 1987). Nonetheless, complaining and "railing against real or imagined slights" (Organ, 1988, p. 11) can certainly occupy supervisory time that might be more productively spent on other activities.

Organizational Courtesy (Organ, 1988) can be characterized by a couple of examples: (a) touching base with the boss to inform him or her about an upcoming situation or event he or she should be aware of to ensure effective response; and

(b) preparing secretaries in advance of a significant future workload increase. Graham (1986) defined *Civic Virtue* as responsible participation in the political life of the organization, for example, attending meetings when it is important to do so. Finally, Hogan and Hogan (1989) and others referred to an employee reliability criterion concept including such behaviors as defying rules, ignoring social expectations, avoiding commitments, and being insubordinate to bosses.

Our taxonomy attempts to summarize OCB, POB, and the other concepts just reviewed into a small number of contextual performance categories. Table 1 contains the five-category system and citations for previously derived concepts contributing to each of the categories.

Our position is that contextual performance is importantly different from task performance in at least three ways. First, task activities vary considerably across jobs whereas contextual activities tend to be more similar across jobs. This has

TABLE 1
Borman and Motowidlo Taxonomy of Contextual Performance

1. Persisting with enthusiasm and extra effort as necessary to complete own task activities successfully.
    - Perseverance and conscientiousness (Borman et al., 1985)
    - Extra effort on the job (Brief & Motowidlo, 1986; Katz & Kahn, 1978)
2. Volunteering to carry out task activities that are not formally part of own job.
    - Suggesting organizational improvements (Brief & Motowidlo, 1986; Katz & Kahn, 1978)
    - Initiative and taking on extra responsibility (Borman et al., 1985; Brief & Motowidlo, 1986; Katz & Kahn, 1978)
    - Making constructive suggestions (George & Brief, 1992)
    - Developing oneself (George & Brief, 1992)
3. Helping and cooperating with others.
    - Assisting/helping coworkers (Borman et al., 1985; Brief & Motowidlo, 1986; Katz & Kahn, 1978)
    - Assisting/helping customers (Brief & Motowidlo, 1986)
    - Organizational courtesy (Organ, 1988)
    - Sportsmanship (Organ, 1988)
    - Altruism (Smith et al., 1983)
    - Helping coworkers (George & Brief, 1992)
4. Following organizational rules and procedures.
    - Following orders and regulations and respect for authority (Borman et al., 1985)
    - Complying with organizational values and policies (Brief & Motowidlo, 1986)
    - Conscientiousness (Smith et al., 1983)
    - Meeting deadlines (Katz & Kahn, 1978)
    - Civic virtue (Graham, 1986)
5. Endorsing, supporting, and defending organizational objectives
    - Organizational loyalty (Graham, 1986)
    - Concern for unit objectives (Borman et al., 1985)
    - Staying with the organization during hard times and representing the organization favorably to outsiders (Brief & Motowidlo, 1986)
    - Protecting the organization (George & Brief, 1992)

implications we discuss later. Second, task activities are more likely than contextual activities to be role-prescribed, for example, to appear on a performance appraisal form. A study by Conway (1996) supported this assertion. When Conway had a small panel of Industrial/Organizational psychologists sort performance dimensions from 14 mutitrait multimethod matrices that appeared in the literature into the task or contextual domain, 55% were reliably identified as task dimension, 30% as contextual dimensions, and there was disagreement about 15%. This study also shows that the task-contextual distinction is not always clear. Third, antecedents of task performance are more likely to involve cognitive ability, whereas antecedents of contextual performance are more likely to involve personality variables.

The latter point is the main theme of this article. If we include as criteria contextual performance factors, then personality predictors will be more successful in personnel selection research than if these factors are not included. In fact, we believe that when personality has predicted job performance, often the criteria have contained elements of contextual performance. For example, in meta-analyses of personality scale validities against job performance (Barrick & Mount, 1991; Tett, Jackson, & Rothstein, 1991), the moderate correlations may be a function of the personality predictors correlating with the contextual elements of performance when the criterion measures were overall performance ratings (which they often were). This is because it can be demonstrated that overall job performance ratings, used in the majority of selection studies (e.g., Landy & Farr, 1983), are influenced substantially by ratees' contextual performance. The next section provides evidence for this assertion.

IMPACT OF RATEE CONTEXTUAL PERFORMANCE ON OVERALL PERFORMANCE RATINGS

Several studies have shown that ratee contextual performance has a significant impact on overall performance ratings. For example, MacKenzie, Podsakoff, and Fetter (1991) had sales managers' supervisory ratings of insurance agents' overall performance and their OCB. Agent sales data were also available. Regression analyses were conducted with the overall performance ratings as the dependent variable, and sales data, arguably an index of task performance, and OCB, an element of contextual performance, as independent variables. Beta weights for the independent variables were both significant and roughly equal in magnitude, suggesting that these supervisors weighted task and contextual performance about the same in making overall performance judgments.

In a second study (Motowidlo & Van Scotter, 1994), about 300 Air Force first-termers were each rated by three supervisors. One rater made an overall performance rating, a second provided ratings on task performance, and a third rated contextual performance using the Borman and Motowidlo taxonomy to define the dimensions. The correlation between the task performance and overall performance ratings was .43. The correlation between contextual performance and overall performance ratings was .41. Again, the inference can be made that supervisory ratings are a function of both task and contextual performance.

Third, Borman, White, and Dorsey (1995) had supervisors and peers of more than 400 first-tour soldiers making ratings on interpersonal factors related to friendliness, dependability, and obnoxiousness. A second set of supervisors and peers made overall performance ratings. Also available for ratees were work sample and job knowledge test scores. Path analyses showed for the supervisor model that ratee dependability, a contextual factor, and work sample performance, a task-related factor, had the largest (and equal) path coefficients to the overall ratings variable. Results were similar with the peer model except that the obnoxiousness-overall ratings path was also significant (and negative). Both models again provide evidence for overall performance ratings being a function of both task and contextual performance. Other research has reported similar results: (a) Werner's (1994) study of the impact of in-role and extra-role behavior on supervisory ratings; (b) Van Scotter and Motowidlo's (1996) research on the relation between overall performance ratings and ratings on task performance and on two contextual factors; and (c) the Ferris, Judge, Rowland, and Fitzgibbons (1994) study, testing a model of subordinate influence on supervisory ratings.

Accordingly, it appears well-established that global overall performance ratings are influenced substantially by ratee contextual performance. This becomes important in providing an alternative explanation for the current strong stance that personality predicts job performance (e.g., Hogan, Hogan, & Roberts, 1996). If ratings are used as criteria (as they often are) in establishing this personality–job performance link, then it may be that personality predictors are actually linked to the contextual performance element of those ratings. This becomes a more plausible explanation when we demonstrate in the next section of this article that personality does in fact have significant links to contextual performance.

EVIDENCE THAT PERSONALITY PREDICTS CONTEXTUAL PERFORMANCE

A meta-analytic review and several individual studies provide evidence for personality predicting contextual-related performance. Regarding the meta-analysis, Kamp and Hough (1988) examined correlations between measures of eight personality constructs and a variety of criteria such as job proficiency, school success, training performance, and delinquency. The criterion conceptually closest to contextual performance was delinquency. In military studies, it was indexed by such measures as AWOLs and unfavorable discharges; in nonmilitary studies discipline criteria included number of violations of company policy and employee theft. In the meta-analysis, mean corrected (for restriction-in-range) correlations were substantial for the two personality constructs conceptually closest to this criterion. These mean correlations were –.42 for predictor scales classified as measuring adjustment (across four studies with a total N ≈ 5,600), and –.43 for scales identified as measuring dependability (employing nine studies with a total $N = 10{,}000$). Also, the correlations between personality and this contextual criterion were in general much higher than between personality and the other criteria that did not appear to represent contextual performance.

As part of Project A, the large-scale test validation research effort conducted in the U.S. Army (e.g., Campbell, 1990), three summary personality factors were among several predictor measures developed for the project. In addition, five summary criterion constructs consistently emerged from the criterion research done on first-tour soldiers. One of the five, *Core Technical Proficiency,* is unambiguously a task performance factor, and another dimension, *Personal Discipline,* is clearly a contextual factor. Results of a concurrent validation study conducted as part of Project A are depicted in Table 2. General cognitive ability, measured by the Armed Services Vocational Aptitude Battery, correlated substantially higher with the task performance dimension than with the contextual dimension. This pattern is reversed at least in part for the personality predictors. Most notably, *Dependability* has a clearly more substantial relation with the contextual factor than it does with the task factor.

The Motowidlo and Van Scotter (1994) article, discussed previously, also had data relevant to the point that personality constructs are good predictors of contextual performance. Table 3 contains the correlations between the personality predictors from that study and the task and contextual performance ratings provided by supervisors. In general, correlations between these personality scales and the contextual performance ratings are higher than those with the task performance ratings. This pattern is clearest for Work Orientation, Dependability, Cooperativeness, and Locus of Control, where the personality–contextual performance correlations are significantly different from the personality–task performance correlations ($p < .05$, one-tailed). Again, although the pattern is not evident for some personality predictors, the general finding is that personality correlates more highly with contextual performance than with task performance.

TABLE 2
Selected Project A Predictor–Criterion Correlations

Predictors	*Core Technical Proficiency*	*Personal Discipline*
General Cognitive Ability	.33	.08
Achievement	.11	.18
Dependability	.11	.30
Adjustment	.10	.11

Note. $n = 4{,}039$.

TABLE 3
Personality–Criterion Performance Correlations From Motowidlo and Van Scotter (1994)

Predictors	*Task Performance*	*Contextual Performance*
Work Orientation	.23	.36
Dominance	.04	.11
Dependability	.18	.31
Adjustment	.08	.14
Cooperativeness	.03	.22
Internal Locus of Control	.08	.26

Note. $n = 252–256$.

Still another study investigated relations between two prosocial personality dimensions and OCB. Penner, Fritzsche, Craiger, and Friefield (1995) developed a self-report inventory that measures two personality constructs: Other-Oriented Empathy and Helpfulness. The former is intended to tap the tendency to have prosocial thoughts and feelings; the latter is intended to tap the tendency to engage in prosocial acts. Recently, Midili and Penner (1995) found that Other-Oriented Empathy correlated .36 with self-ratings of OCB and Helpfulness correlated .42 with this measure of OCB. The relations held when social desirability was partialled out of both measures.

Finally, validation research conducted using the Hogan Personality Inventory (HPI) provided an opportunity to examine more directly the notion that personality scale scores may be more closely linked to contextual performance than to overall performance. In 13 of the 14 validation studies with the HPI done from 1993 to 1996 (total $N = 1{,}156$), the mean correlations between scores on the seven basic HPI scales (e.g., Adjustment, Ambition, etc.) and ratings on contextual criteria such as teamwork, customer service, and resolving conflict were higher than correlations between these scales and the overall performance rating criteria. Admittedly, this is a crude comparison. The number of studies is small and the contextual criterion dimensions were linked to individual HPI scales according to conceptual matches to obtain the mean personality–contextual performance correlations. However, results were reasonably consistent, with the weighted mean difference between correlations with contextual criteria and overall performance criteria equal to .08.

These findings suggest that when the contextual components of overall performance can be measured separately, personality predictor validities will be higher than when the criterion is overall performance. The bandwidth–fidelity issue in predicting behavior may also be relevant here.

Briefly, an additional reason HPI scales may correlate more highly with contextual-like criteria is the similarity in their bandwidths. The HPI basic scales probably target a criterion domain more narrow than overall performance. In fact, Hogan and Roberts (in press) made a strong case for global overall performance having a wider bandwidth than personality scales in general. Accordingly, from both a predictor-criterion conceptual matching perspective (e.g., Schneider, Hough, & Dunnette, in press) and a bandwidth similarity perspective, typical personality scales should relate more highly with contextual performance factors than with overall performance.

Thus, we return to our alternative interpretation of studies demonstrating validity for personality predictors when overall performance ratings or a composite of ratings on several dimensions are the criterion measure. Research reviewed in the previous section strongly suggests that these global ratings are a function of both task and contextual performance on the part of ratees. This section has presented considerable evidence for substantial personality–contextual performance linkages. Accordingly, we again propose that significant correlations between personality constructs and "job performance" in meta-analyses, for example, where most criteria were overall performance ratings, are a result of personality primarily correlating with the contextual components of those ratings.

CONCLUSIONS

There are three major conclusions we would draw from the discussion here. First, in our judgment, the contextual performance domain is important—it seems conceptually, and to some extent at least, empirically distinct from the task performance domain. In fact, we believe that in the future (a) as global competition continues to raise the effort levels required of employees, (b) as team-based organizations become even more popular, (c) as downsizing continues to make employee adaptability and willingness to exhibit extra effort more of a necessity, (d) as customer service is increasingly emphasized, and (e) as fields of work in part at least replace jobs as the envelope of work, contextual performance will become more and more important in organizations. Second, research shows that experienced supervisors consider contextual performance on the part of subordinates when making overall performance ratings. A consistent finding is that supervisors weight contextual performance approximately as highly as task performance in making these judgments. And finally, very important for personnel selection, when contextual performance dimensions are included as criteria, personality predictors are more likely to be successful correlates. We have seen this fairly clear-cut pattern of validities, especially in Project A; the Motowidlo and Van Scotter (1994) research; and the Midili and Penner (1995) study, where personality predicts performance in the contextual domain. As discussed earlier, these results may help explain recent meta-analytic findings—for example Barrick and Mount's (1991) demonstration of consistent, moderate-level correlations between the Big 5 personality dimension Conscientiousness and job performance. The personality measures may be picking up on the contextual component of the criteria. This implies that where the contextual elements of performance can be measured separately, these personality-performance validities might be higher.

In fact, that is our strong hypothesis. If, for example, we could conduct a meta-analysis of personality validities similar to Barrick and Mount, but with studies included only if the criteria were identified as contextual in nature, our prediction is that the results would be more favorable to personality predictors.

In sum, we argued for the importance of contextual activities as performance criteria. These criterion elements can be distinguished from task activities, and they appear important for organizational effectiveness, with organizational and business trends likely to make contextual performance even more important in the future. In addition, evidence was presented demonstrating that measures of personality constructs correlate substantially with contextual criterion measures. More broadly, evidence toward establishing empirical links between personality constructs and relatively specific criterion constructs contributes importantly to the science of personnel selection.

REFERENCES

Barnard, C. I. (1938). *The functions of the executive.* Cambridge, MA: Harvard University Press.

Barrick, M. R., & Mount, M. K. (1991). The big five personality dimensions and job performance: A meta-analysis. *Personnel Psychology, 44,* 1–26.

Bateman, T. S., & Organ, D. W. (1983). Job satisfaction and the good soldier: The relationship between affect and employee "citizenship." *Academy of Management Journal, 26,* 587–595.

Borman, W.C., & Motowidlo, S. J. (1993). Expanding the criterion domain to include elements of contextual performance. In N. Schmitt & W. C. Borman (Eds.), *Personnel selection in organizations.* San Francisco: Jossey-Bass.

Borman, W. C., Motowidlo, S. J., Rose, S. R., & Hanser, L. M. (1985). *Development of a model of soldier effectiveness* (Institute Report #95). Minneapolis, MN: Personnel Decisions Research Institutes.

Borman, W. C., White, L. A., & Dorsey, D. W. (1995). Effects of ratee task performance and interpersonal factors on supervisor and peer performance ratings. *Journal of Applied Psychology, 80,* 168–177.

Brief, A. P., & Motowidlo, S. J. (1986). Prosocial organizational behaviors. *Academy of Management Review, 11,* 710–725.

Campbell, J. P. (1990). An overview of the army selection and classification project (Project A). *Personnel Psychology, 43,* 231–239.

Conway, J. M. (1996). Additional construct validity evidence for the task-contextual performance distinction. *Human Performance, 9,* 309–329.

Ferris, G. R., Judge, T. A., Rowland, K. M., & Fitzgibbons, D. E. (1994). Subordinate influence and the performance evaluation process: Test of a model. *Organizational Behavior & Human Decision Processes, 58,* 101–135.

George, J. M., & Brief, A. P. (1992). Feeling good-doing good: A conceptual analysis of the mood at work-organizational spontaneity relationship. *Psychological Bulletin, 112,* 310–329.

Graham, J. W. (1986, August). *Organizational citizenship informed by political theory.* Paper presented at the meeting of the Academy of Management, Chicago.

Hogan, J., & Hogan, R. T. (1989). How to measure employee reliability. *Journal of Applied Psychology, 74,* 273–279.

Hogan, R. T., Hogan, J., & Roberts, B. W. (1996). Personality measurement and employment decisions: Questions and answers. *American Psychologist, 51,* 469–477.

Hogan, J., & Roberts, B. W. (in press). Issues and non-issues in the fidelity/bandwidth tradeoff. *Journal of Organizational Behavior, 17.*

Kamp, J. O., & Hough, L. M. (1988). Utility of temperament for predicting job performance. In L. M. Hough (Ed.), *Literature review: Utility of temperament, biodata, and interest assessment for predicting job performance* (ARI Research Note 88–02). Alexandria, VA: U.S. Army Research Institute for the Behavioral and Social Sciences.

Katz, D. (1964). The motivational basis of organizational behavior. *Behavioral Science, 9,* 131–46.

Katz, D., & Kahn, R. L. (1978). *The social psychology of organizations.* New York: Wiley.

Landy, F. J., & Farr, J. L. (1983). *The measurement of work performance: Methods, theory, and applications.* New York: Academic.

MacKenzie, S. B., Podsakoff, P. M., & Fetter, R. (1991). Organizational citizenship behavior and objective productivity as determinants of managerial evaluations of salespersons' performance. *Organizational Behavior and Human Decisions Processes, 50,* 123–150.

Midili, A. R., & Penner, L. A. (1995, August). *Dispositional and environmental influences on organizational citizenship behavior.* Paper presented at Annual Meeting of the American Psychological Association, New York.

Motowidlo, S. J., & Van Scotter, J. R. (1994). Evidence that task performance should be distinguished from contextual performance. *Journal of Applied Psychology, 79,* 475–80.

Near, J. P., & Miceli, M. P. (1987). Whistle blowers in organizations: Dissidents or reformers? In L. L. Cummings & B. M. Staw (Eds.), *Research in organizational behavior* (Vol. 9, pp. 321–368). Greenwich, CT: JAI.

Organ, D. W. (1988). *Organizational citizenship behavior: The good soldier syndrome.* Lexington, MA: Lexington.

Penner, L. A., Fritzsche, B. A., Craiger, J. P., & Friefield, T. R. (1995). Measuring the prosocial personality. In J. Butcher & C. D. Spielberger (Eds.), *Advances in personality assessment* (Vol. 10, pp. 147–163). Hillsdale, NJ: Lawrence Erlbaum Associates, Inc.

Schneider, R. J., Hough, L. M., & Dunnette, M. D. (in press). Broadsided by broad traits or how to sink science in five dimensions or less. *Journal of Organizational Behavior, 17.*

Smith, C. A., Organ, D. W., & Near, J. P. (1983). Organizational citizenship behavior: Its nature and antecedents. *Journal of Applied Psychology, 68,* 653–663.

Tett, R. P, Jackson, D. N., & Rothstein, M. (1991). Personality measures as predictors of job performance: A meta-analytic review. *Personnel Psychology, 44,* 703–742.

Van Scotter, J. R., & Motowidlo, S. J. (1996). Evidence for two factors of contextual performance: Job dedication and interpersonal facilitation. *Journal of Applied Psychology,* 525–531.

Werner, J. M. (1994). Dimensions that make a difference: Examining the impact of in-role and extra-role behaviors on supervisory ratings. *Journal of Applied Psychology, 79,* 98–107.

HUMAN PERFORMANCE, *10*(2), 111–131

Beyond Job Attitudes: A Personality and Social Psychology Perspective on the Causes of Organizational Citizenship Behavior

Louis A. Penner
Department of Psychology
University of South Florida

Alison R. Midili
Publix Supermarkets

Jill Kegelmeyer
Department of Psychology
University of South Florida

It is a well-established fact that job attitudes and organizational variables are causally related to organizational citizenship behavior (OCB), but it is unlikely that they are the only causes of this important organizational behavior. This article concerns some other possible causes of OCB. On the basis of prior research on OCB and a conceptually related phenomenon—volunteerism—we propose that two kinds of dispositional variables may play significant roles in OCB. The first of these is an individual's motives for engaging in OCB. It is argued that because OCB may serve different needs or motives for different individuals, the measurement of these motives will improve the prediction of OCB. The other dispositional variable is a personality trait—the prosocial personality orientation. Because OCB is a prosocial action and this personality trait involves prosocial thoughts, feelings, and actions, it may predict OCB better than more general personality traits. Data are presented to support the argument that both of the dispositional variables are related to OCB. Finally, it is suggested that engaging in OCB might affect a person's self-concept. Specifically, there is reason to believe it can produce changes in personal identity that are consistent

Requests for reprints should be sent to Louis A. Penner, Department of Psychology, BEH 339, University of South Florida, Tampa, FL 33620–8200.

with the role of an organizational citizen. Role identity and the more psychological variables mentioned earlier are integrated into a model of the causes of enduring OCB. In this model, job attitudes, organizational variables, motives, and personality traits all affect initial levels of OCB. This behavior, in turn, influences the extent to which a person develops a role identity as an organizational citizen. And it is this role identity that directly causes enduring levels of OCB. The utility of this model for predicting OCB and increasing the incidence of this behavior is discussed.

This article examines possible causes of organizational citizenship behavior (OCB). The title suggests our basic thesis. There is little question that both the affective and cognitive components of job attitudes are causally related to OCB. However, we believe there is substantial variance in OCB that cannot be explained by job attitudes, and that other kinds of variables will provide us with a greater understanding of why OCB occurs in the first place, and what sustains it over an extended period of time. These variables are suggested by recent work in the disciplines of personality psychology, social psychology, and sociology on prosocial behaviors in an organizational context.

A substantial portion of this work has been done on volunteerism rather than OCB. Therefore, our first task is to make the case that volunteerism and OCB share enough important attributes that it is reasonable to apply what is known about one phenomenon to the other. In the first section of this article we attempt to do this by identifying some of the similarities and differences among volunteerism, OCB, and other kinds of prosocial behaviors; especially those commonly studied by social and personality psychologists. In the next few sections, we discuss some possible causes of OCB. The discussion begins with job attitudes, but then moves to some dispositional variables that have not, as far as we know, been considered in the OCB literature. Following this, we introduce a sociological theory of the processes that might sustain OCB over an extended period of time. And in the final portion of the article, we integrate all the variables that we have discussed into a conceptual model of the direct and indirect causes of enduring OCB.

ORGANIZATIONAL CITIZENSHIP AS A PROSOCIAL BEHAVIOR

OCB is a cluster of behaviors that benefit an organization and/or groups and individuals within it. The term *Conscientiousness* (or Compliance) is used to describe OCB that is directed at the organization; the term *Altruism* is used to describe OCB that is directed at individuals within the organization (Organ, 1988; Smith, Organ, & Near, 1983). Although the Altruism dimension of OCB would appear to be conceptually equivalent to the kinds of prosocial behaviors commonly studied by social psychologists, a closer inspection suggests that this may not always be the case.

As most readers are aware, among social psychologists there is a long and very active interest in when and why people act prosocially (Schroeder, Penner, Dovidio, & Piliavin, 1995). However, until relatively recently, the primary focus of interest was on a very specific form of prosocial action—bystanders intervening to offer help to a physically distressed stranger. Social psychologists' interest in this aspect of prosocial behavior can be traced almost directly to the now famous (or infamous) "Kitty Genovese Incident" and the seminal research on bystander intervention of Latané and Darley (1970). The central question addressed by Latané and Darley was why the people who witnessed the assault and murder of Ms. Genovese failed to intervene on her behalf. Thus, for several years, bystander intervention (or the apparent absence of it) was the aspect of prosocial behavior that captured the attention of most social psychologists.

There is some overlap between bystander intervention and the Altruism dimension of OCB, but there are many differences between them as well. Let us first consider the most important communalities between the two kinds of prosocial actions. Bystander interventions are one aspect of Altruism. That is, Altruism can include single acts of helping intended to benefit another person with a specific transitory problem. These particular kinds of OCBs are spontaneous, short-term, and primarily determined by the characteristics of the situation in which a potential helper is placed. Thus, to understand one aspect of OCB, we need to be aware of the variables that affect bystander interventions. The social psychological literature identifies many of these variables. Among them are the potential helper's affect and cognitions at the time help is needed, the current and prior relation between the potential helper and the potential recipient, and the personal and demographic characteristics of both the helper and the recipient (see Schroeder et al., 1995, chap. 9).

However, there is much more to OCB than people's spontaneous reactions to one-time crises in the lives of their coworkers. Thus, we must search for other kinds of prosocial behavior that might have more in common with OCB than bystander intervention. As suggested earlier, we believe that a good candidate is the phenomenon of volunteerism. According to Hanson (1991), volunteering is a "form of formal planned helping" that typically involves giving time to help others through organizations such as churches, schools, hospitals, and service organizations (also see Allen, 1982). Hanson proposed that three characteristics distinguish volunteerism from bystander intervention, and, in our view, make it quite similar to OCB.

First, whereas bystander intervention is a short-lived phenomenon, volunteerism often involves a relatively long-term commitment. Second, bystander intervention involves an immediate reaction to a specific situation; volunteerism, on the other hand, involves a thoughtful decision to seek out a situation in which the volunteer can provide help. Third, bystander intervention typical occurs in an interpersonal context, but volunteerism occurs in an organizational context. That is, most volunteers work for some service organization. Finally, whereas situational factors or personal relationships may sometimes seem to force bystanders into intervening, volunteering is almost by definition "sustained helping without obligation" (Omoto & Snyder, 1995, p. 671). People choose to be volunteers; they are not required to do this because of personal or professional relationships.

Now let us consider the defining characteristics of OCB. Usually, it is defined as extra-role behaviors that may benefit an organization or people within the organization, but these behaviors are not part of a worker's formal job description or requirements. That is, people voluntarily choose to engage in OCB (Borman & Motowidlo, 1993; Organ, 1988; Organ & Ryan, 1995). Like volunteerism, OCB is a long-term behavior that typically involves proactive efforts to benefit others, and takes place in an organizational setting. The fact that OCB is a voluntary, extra-role behavior does not mean that OCB goes unnoticed and unappreciated by an organization's leaders, that it has no impact on formal and informal evaluations of an employee's performance, or even that people are unaware of the benefits that might result from being a good organizational citizen. To the contrary, there is evidence that OCB is noticed, does affect evaluations, and that workers know this (Allen, 1996; Borman, White, & Dorsey, 1995; Motowidlo & Van Scotter, 1994). However, the perspective taken in this article is that people engage in both OCB and in volunteerism because they want to rather than because they are formally required to. Thus, the defining characteristic of OCB is not that it is prosocial and selfless, but rather that it is prosocial and voluntary.[1]

In summary, we view OCB as a form of prosocial behavior that contains some of the elements of short-term, spontaneous bystander interventions. However, OCB is conceptually and operationally much more similar to volunteerism. Thus, studies concerned with volunteerism may inform us about the causes of OCBs and vice-versa. We consider the results of some volunteerism studies shortly, but now we turn to the causes of OCB.

JOB ATTITUDES AND OCB

In a recent meta-analysis of the OCB literature, Organ and Ryan (1995) identified several variables as causes of OCB. Chief among these was job attitudes. Most models of the structure of an attitude posit that it has two components: cognitive, or thoughts about the attributes of the attitude object; and affective, or feelings about the attitude object (Eagly & Chaiken, 1993). It is widely accepted that both components of workers' attitudes toward their job play a critical causal role in OCB (Organ & Ryan, 1995).

[1]The absence of an altruistic motive does not distinguish OCB from most prosocial behaviors. To the contrary, there are numerous models of prosocial behavior that argue it is primarily motivated by egoistic and self-serving concerns (e.g., Cialdini, 1991; Dovidio, Piliavin, Gaertner, Schroeder, & Clark, 1991).

Cognitions and OCB

Workers who are satisfied with their jobs and believe they have been treated fairly are more likely to engage in OCB than workers who are dissatisfied and believe they have been treated unfairly or unjustly (Organ & Ryan, 1995).[2] Social exchange theory (Thibaut & Kelley, 1959) provides a parsimonious explanation of why job satisfaction apparently leads to OCB. This classic social psychological theory proposes that human interactions can be conceptualized as business transactions in which people exchange resources in the hope that they will earn profits. The key to a successful (i.e., profitable) exchange relationship is reciprocity, in which one party to the relationship gives some resource to the other and the recipient responds in kind. However, sometimes workers may receive certain resources (e.g., a raise, kind treatment from a supervisor), but the nature of their job is such that they cannot reciprocate by improving their productivity or other aspects of their formal task performance. Therefore, they may choose to reciprocate by providing another resource that is under their control—OCB.

The term used to describe fair treatment of a worker in an organizational context is *organizational justice.* It refers to workers' perceptions that they are being treated fairly with regard to things such as the distribution of the rewards they receive and the procedures used to make decisions that affect them. Equity theory (Adams, 1965; Walster, Walster, & Berscheid, 1978) explains the positive association between perceived organizational justice and OCB (Organ & Ryan, 1995). The basic premise of equity theory is that people expect to be treated fairly in their exchanges with others. People will see a relationship as fair or equitable if the outcomes they receive from the relationship match their contributions to it. If people feel that they have been treated fairly, they will want to treat the other parties to the relationship fairly—either because of a concern about how the other parties might react to inequitable treatment or to ensure that the relationship will continue to produce this fair ratio of outcomes and contributions. If a worker's outcomes exceed his or her contributions and the person cannot restore equity within the context of the formal job requirements, engaging in OCB would become a means to restore equity (Organ, 1990; Organ & Konovsky; 1989).

Although most studies find positive associations between organizational justice and OCB, they have used a cross-sectional methodology. This makes it difficult, if not impossible, to make strong causal inferences about organizational justice and OCB. To infer a causal relation between two variables there must be reliable covariation between them, temporal precedence of the presumed cause over the

[2]It could be reasonably argued that job satisfaction is part of the affective component of job attitudes. However, most operationalizations of this construct (e.g., the Job Descriptive Index) assess cognitions about specific facets of a job.

presumed effect, and sufficient control of other possible causal variables to rule out alternative interpretations of a cause and effect relation (Cook & Campbell, 1979). Only the first of these conditions is met in a cross-sectional study. There are, however, some more recent findings that speak to the causal relation between organizational justice and OCB.

Wright (1996) conducted a laboratory analogue experiment that examined the impact of one aspect of procedural justice on OCB. Participants in an experiment were treated fairly or unfairly with regard to the number of extra credit points they received for their participation. Shortly thereafter, they were asked to engage in an extra-role behavior that would benefit someone who was associated with the organization that sponsored the study, but was in no way a party to this particular experiment. Specifically, they were asked to help out another experimenter by adding up sets of numbers. The dependent measure was the length of time they worked on this task. Wright found that those who had been treated fairly engaged in significantly more extra-role helping than did those who were treated unfairly.

In another, perhaps more ecologically valid study, Skarlicki and Latham (1996) conducted a quasi-experiment in which one group of union leaders were trained in the skills needed to implement the principles of organizational justice, whereas another group did not receive the training. Later, Skarlicki and Latham obtained self-reports of perceived fairness from the subordinates of both groups of leaders and peer-ratings of the subordinates' OCB. Union members whose leaders received the justice training perceived these leaders as fairer. Peer ratings also indicated that they engaged in a higher level of OCB than did members of the group where the leaders had no training. These two studies provide some degree of empirical support for the notion that organizational justice causes OCBs.

Affect and OCB

The affective component of job attitudes is also related to OCB. For example, positive mood is correlated with higher self- and supervisor-ratings of OCB (George, 1991; George & Brief, 1992; Midili, 1995). The same thing appears to be true for volunteer activities. Penner and Finkelstein (1996) found that affective reactions to the experience of being a volunteer were significantly correlated with contemporaneous reports of the amount of time volunteers spent working for a service organization. Thus, mood, which George and Brief (1992) believed is conceptually distinct from satisfaction with specific aspects of a job, is positively associated with sustained, nonobligated prosocial actions. There are, however, certain issues that must be resolved before we can claim to understand why positive moods are associated with OCB.

First, most of the findings on mood and OCB come from cross-sectional studies; as noted earlier, causality cannot be inferred from cross-sectional data. Moreover, practical and ethical considerations make it unlikely that researchers will be able to use real organizations to conduct experimental or quasi-experimental studies in which mood is systematically manipulated. Wright (1996) attempted to overcome this problem by constructing a laboratory analog to study the mood–OCB relation, but his results were inconclusive.

However, even if we accept the reasonable assumption that mood causes OCB, there is a second problem. It concerns finding a theory or model that might explain the impact of mood on OCB. Equity and social exchange theory provide quite reasonable explanations of why satisfaction and perceived fairness apparently lead to OCB, but they are somewhat less applicable to the mood–OCB relation. George and Brief (1992) recognized this and turned to other social psychological theories of why positive moods lead to increases in prosocial actions.

For example, Isen and her colleagues (Isen, 1993; Isen, Clark, & Schwartz, 1976) proposed that people in a positive mood have a more positive outlook in life and, thus, they may think more about the rewards of helping others than the costs of offering this help. Therefore the perceived incentives for OCB may be greater among people in a positive mood. Carlson, Charlin, and Miller (1988) offered another explanation of how mood affects helping. They argued that people in positive moods desire to maintain these moods. Helping others may serve to maintain this affective state because, among adults, low-cost helping usually improves people's mood. George and Brief suggested that engaging in OCB may serve a similar function because it increases the likelihood that a person will be working in a positive and healthy environment.

Although these and similar explanations seem reasonable, there is one cautionary note. All of them were originally developed to explain transitory increases in helping rather than the long-term and planful kind of helping that is characteristic of most OCB. Thus, the fit between the general theory and the specific phenomenon of interest is good, but it is certainly not perfect.

Despite these conceptual and theoretical ambiguities, it appears that both the cognitive and affective components of job attitudes are, indeed, causally related to OCB. In addition, other closely related constructs, such as leader supportiveness, or leader consideration, also lead to OCB. However, usually the effect sizes for these variables as predictors of OCB are rather small (Organ & Ryan, 1995). To be sure, one reason for this is the typical problems one encounters when measuring these kinds of variables (i.e., less-than-perfect reliability and construct validity in the measures). However, we believe another more substantive reason for the large residual variance is that attitudes toward one's job and the behavior of one's supervisors are not the only significant causes of OCB. In the sections that follow we posit some of the other causes of OCB, discuss the theories that may explain why they affect OCB, and present data in support of the theories. However, as suggested earlier, we must turn to the volunteerism literature to explain why we believe these variables play an important role in OCB.

A FUNCTIONAL APPROACH TO VOLUNTEERISM

The functional approach to volunteerism was developed by Snyder, Omoto, and their colleagues (Clary & Snyder, 1991; Omoto & Snyder, 1995; Omoto, Snyder, & Berghuis, 1993). The material that follows draws heavily from their work. The functional explanation of why some people volunteer their time and energy to a service organization proposes that, "different people can and do engage in the same behaviors for different reasons, in pursuit of different ends, and to serve different psychological functions" (Omoto & Snyder, 1995, p. 673). As Snyder (1993) noted, this view of human motivation is not a new one; it can be directly traced back to the functionalists of the late nineteenth century, such as John Dewey and William James. The central question asked by the functionalist is: What need is being met by the behavior in question?

We can use an OCB to illustrate this point. Imagine that an experienced supervisor at a large technology firm volunteers to stay after work and teach a new subordinate how to use a particular piece of complex software. This seems to be a clear example of an OCB, but from a functional perspective the critical question is: Why has the OCB occurred? The functionalist would argue that we cannot completely answer this question without knowing the functions this behavior would serve for the supervisor. She or he might, for example, feel that she has a personal responsibility to help new workers succeed in their job. In this instance, the behavior has an altruistic motive; it serves to express the helper's values about helping others. However, another supervisor might engage in the same behavior because it serves to show his or her superiority over the new worker; a third supervisor might do this because even though this action is clearly not part of his or her formal job description, he or she feels that supervisors are obligated to do these kinds of things for their subordinates; and a fourth might perform this act because of her or his positive feelings toward the organization and the belief that helping the new worker will benefit the organization. In this example, the helpers' job attitudes would be the relevant motive for the behavior for only one of four supervisors. Thus, if only job attitudes were measured, there would be large amounts of unexplained variance in OCB. However, if these other motives had been measured, we might be able to better understand who would and would not engage in this OCB.

As noted earlier, we are not aware of any specific applications of the functional approach to the prediction of OCB, but there have been at least four studies that have used motives to predict volunteerism (Clary & Orenstein, 1991; Deaux & Stark, 1996; Omoto & Snyder, 1995; Penner & Finkelstein, 1996). For example, Penner and Finkelstein (1996) found that an altruistic, value-based motivation for volunteering predicted how much contact, in a volunteer capacity, male AIDS volunteers had with a person with AIDS 10 months after this motive was measured. The same kind of relation was found by Deaux and Stark (1996) in a study of volunteers working with prisoners and by Clary and Orenstein (1991) in a study of volunteer crisis counselors. On the other hand, Omoto and Snyder (1995) found that self-centered motives predicted the length of time people served as AIDS volunteers.

One implication of the functional approach to prosocial behavior is that if one knows the motives that are most important to an individual, one can maximize the effectiveness of attempts to elicit prosocial behaviors by developing persuasive appeals that target the motives most important to the recipient of the appeal. There is some evidence that persuasive appeals directed at potential volunteers are most effective when they match the target person's reasons for volunteering (Clary et al., 1996; Clary, Snyder, Ridge, Meine, & Haugen, 1994). Also, Clary et al. (1996) found that if volunteers received feedback about aspects of their performance that matched their original motives for volunteering, they tended to be more satisfied with the volunteer experience. Presumably, they also were better and more active volunteers.

These results need to be replicated and extended, but they do suggest that it may be possible to directly affect the incidence of OCB with a functional approach. The first step in doing this would be to identify and then measure the needs that might be most often met by workers engaging in OCB. The volunteerism literature may be instructive in this regard. Clary and Snyder (1991) posited that volunteering might serve four distinct functions. The first is value-expressive, the behavior is motivated by values about other people's well-being. The remaining three motives or functions are: social adjustment—the behavior is motivated by a desire to fit in and be accepted by one's reference group; ego-defensive—the behavior is motivated by a desire to protect yourself from feeling that you are a selfish or uncaring person who does not deserve to have good things happen to him or her; and knowledge—gaining additional knowledge of the world or specific skills associated with the volunteer experience. More recently, Clary et al. (1996) added two more possible motives for volunteerism: career—the activity may prepare the person for a new career; and enhancement—the activity may increase the volunteer's self-esteem and sense of worth.

Attempts to increase OCB that are based on a functional approach might be considerably more effective and efficient than those that seek to increase OCB primarily by changing the affective and cognitive components of general job attitudes. We suggest this because it is well established in the attitude literature that: (a) outside of laboratory settings it is usually quite difficult to change established attitudes, and (b) the link between general attitudes and specific behaviors is rather weak (Eagly & Chaiken, 1993).

The possibility that people might differ with regard to what motivates them to help an organization and individuals within it does not preclude another possibility; namely, that there are also some underlying communalities among people in the reasons why they engage in OCB. That is, OCB may also be influenced by more general dispositional variables that people share in common. If so, then we might be able to add to "the variance accounted for" in the prediction of OCB by considering where people fall in the distributions for certain personality traits. In the next section we review prior research on the personality correlates of OCB and present some specific personality traits that may be related to OCB.

PERSONALITY AND OCB

From almost the beginning of interest in OCB and other extra-role aspects of job performance, researchers expected that individual differences in personality characteristics would result in variability in these behaviors (Borman & Motowidlo, 1993; Organ, 1993). These expectations were based primarily on what personality psychologists have learned about the conditions under which the relation between personality variables and relevant behaviors should be the strongest. Specifically, personality characteristics are most likely to be manifested in overt behaviors when the behaviors involve planful actions, occur over an extended period of time and wide range of situations, and are relatively unconstrained by situational demands or formal role requirements (Funder, 1994). OCB would appear to be reflect such behavior.

Unfortunately these expectations have not been supported by empirical findings on the relation between personality variables and OCB. In their meta-analysis of the precursors of OCB, Organ and Ryan (1995) examined the results of studies that examined the correlations between certain personality variables and OCB. The personality variables included were the Agreeableness and Conscientiousness factors from the Five-Factor Model of Personality (Costa & McCrae, 1992) and Negative Affectivity and Positive Affectivity (Watson & Clark, 1992); the criterion measures were peer or supervisor ratings of the Altruism and Conscientiousness dimensions of OCB. Across the studies, Agreeableness had the largest average correlation with the Altruism dimension of OCB (r = .10). The largest average correlation for the OCB dimension of Conscientiousness was with the personality trait of Conscientiousness; it was .23.[3] The average rs between OCB and both measures of affectivity were .15 or less. These results led Organ and Ryan (1995) to conclude that if personality characteristics play any role in OCB, it is probably an indirect one. Specifically, they argued that, "Disposition enters into this scheme (i.e., predicts OCB) to the extent that differences in innate temperament or stable personality factors, directly or indirectly, contribute to (a general morale) factor" (1995, p. 795).

They did allow that the trait Conscientiousness might directly predict certain aspects of OCB, and they acknowledged there were many other potential personality correlates of OCB that had not yet been studied. However, overall Organ and

[3]These correlations would be somewhat larger if studies that used self-ratings of OCB were included.

Ryan were rather pessimistic about the possibility that individual differences in personality might directly account for significant variation in OCB.

We do not share this pessimism about the utility of personality variables in the prediction of OCB. To explain the basis of our disagreement and to provide a context for some empirical findings that we will report, we need to digress from the main focus of this article and discuss the work of Louis A. Penner and his associates on the prosocial personality orientation.

THE PROSOCIAL PERSONALITY ORIENTATION

In the early 1990s, Penner and his colleagues began to develop a scale that measured a prosocial personality orientation—an enduring predisposition to feel concern about the welfare of other people, to think about their best interests, and to engage in actions on their behalf. They used electronic databases (e.g., PsychLit) and manual literature searches to identify all the personality scales that previously had been found to correlate with prosocial affect, cognitions, and actions (most commonly helping). There were many such scales, but a scale was considered for inclusion only if it met a second selection criterion—there was a theory or model of helping that would explain why the personality characteristic measured by this scale was associated with prosocial tendencies. Thus, for example, measures of empathy were included because in almost every major theory of why people offer aid, empathic reactions are identified as a crucial mediational variable (see Schroeder et al., 1995). Measures of Machiavellianism, however, were excluded because there was no theory of helping that explained why this trait would affect prosocial responses.

The selected scales were included in their entirety in a 128-item initial version of the Prosocial Personality Battery (PSB; see Penner, Fritzsche, Craiger, & Freifeld, 1995). Certain scales and some individual items in other scales were then removed from the PSB on the basis of correlations with independent measures of prosocial thoughts, feelings, and actions, and item-remainder correlations. The result of this was the 56-item final version of the PSB. The scales included in the PSB assess the propensity to: experience affective empathy (Empathic Concern), cognitive empathy (Perspective Taking), and egocentric or self-oriented empathy (Personal Distress; items from Davis, 1980); feel responsibility for one's own actions and the welfare of others (items from Schwartz & Howard, 1982); use certain rules when making moral decisions (original items written for the PSB, based on Gilligan, 1982); and offer help to needy individuals and groups (items from Rushton, Chrisjohn, & Fekken, 1981).

Penner and Craiger (1991) conducted a principal axis factor analysis of the scales that make up the PSB. A Promax (oblique) rotation yielded a theoretically coherent and interpretable two-factor solution. The first factor is called Other-Oriented

Empathy: the tendency to experience empathy for, and to feel responsibility and concern about, the well-being of others; in other words, prosocial thoughts and feelings. The second factor is called Helpfulness: a self-reported history of engaging in helpful actions and an absence of egocentric physical reactions to other's distress; in other words, prosocial behavior. The two factor scores (derived by summing total scores on the scales that have their primary loading on that factor) correlate .10 to .40 depending on the sample. The factors are internally consistent (alphas in excess of .80) and temporally stable (4-week test–retest reliabilities .77 and .85, respectively). The factor structure is invariant across gender and includes samples from different regions of the United States and people with differing levels of education.[4]

Penner et al. (1995) conducted a number of studies that suggest the two dimensions are, in fact, correlated with several different aspects of prosocial behavior in an interpersonal context; included among these are the number of helpful acts college students performed over a 1-month period of time, affective reactions to people in distress, and estimates of the costs of helping such people. However, the findings of most direct interest here come from research on OCB conducted by Alison R. Midili (Midili, 1995; Midili & Penner, 1995).

In the first of two studies, employees of a large retail store anonymously filled out measures of mood, job satisfaction, the PSB, and a scale developed by Midili to measure the Altruism and Conscientiousness dimensions of OCB (Midili & Penner, 1995). Other-Oriented Empathy correlated significantly with both of the OCB dimensions and Helpfulness correlated significantly with the Altruism dimension of OCB.[5] Midili and Penner also conducted a hierarchical multiple regression in which the two dimensions of the PSB were entered after the measures of mood and job satisfaction. Each of the PSB dimensions accounted for significant unique variance in the prediction of Altruism; Other-Oriented Empathy also accounted for significant unique variance in Conscientiousness.

Midili (1995) replicated and extended these findings. She again measured mood and administered the PSB, but she replaced the measure of job satisfaction with measures of different aspects of organizational justice. Also, in this study Midili obtained self, peer, and supervisor ratings of OCB. (The OCB measure was a shortened version of the OCB scale developed by Podsakoff & MacKenzie, 1989.) The earlier results for the self-reports of OCB were replicated almost exactly. That is, both dimensions of the PSB were significantly correlated with Altruism scores; Other-Oriented Empathy correlated significantly with the Conscientiousness dimension of the OCB scale; and Other-Oriented Empathy and Helpfulness each accounted for unique variance in the hierarchical multiple regressions that predicted the Altruism dimension even when they were entered after the organizational justice

[4]A complete copy of the PSB and scoring instructions are available from Louis A. Penner.

[5]These correlations remained significant even after social desirability was partialled out.

and mood measures. Other-Oriented Empathy also accounted for unique variance in the prediction of Conscientiousness.

Obviously, these findings are limited by the fact that they only involved self-reports of OCB. Thus, some of the covariation among the dimensions of the PSB and the OCB measures might reflect some common method or rater variance. The peers' ratings of the employees' OCB eliminated these problems to a considerable extent.

Other-Oriented Empathy and Helpfulness were both significantly correlated with the peers' ratings of the target persons on the Altruism and Conscientiousness dimensions of the OCB scale. Once again hierarchical multiple regressions were conducted in which the PSB dimensions were entered into the hierarchical regression after the other measures (i.e., mood and organizational justice). Other-Oriented Empathy and Helpfulness were the only variables that accounted for significant variance in peer ratings of Altruism. One aspect of organizational justice (interactional justice—how the participants thought they were treated by their supervisors) accounted for significant variance on the Conscientiousness dimension, but Other-Oriented Empathy and Helpfulness accounted for unique additional variance when they were entered into the regression equation.

These positive findings for the personality measure were not obtained for the supervisor ratings. Although the justice measures and mood did have significant zero-order correlations with the supervisors' ratings of overall OCB and Altruism, none of the zero-order correlations among the PSB dimensions and the OCB ratings even approached statistical significance. We have no ready explanation of why the personality measures were unrelated to the supervisors' ratings of OCB; however, a study by McNeely and Meglino (1994) suggested one possibility. They used personality measures somewhat similar to the PSB dimensions and found that the personality variables predicted OCB directed at specific individuals, whereas measures of justice and equity predicted OCB directed at the organization. Thus, even though the peers and the supervisors in Midili's second study used exactly the same rating form, they may have based their ratings on different aspects of the target employees' extra-role prosocial extra role behaviors.

The disparity between the findings for the self- and peer-ratings of OCB and the supervisors' ratings is something that should be pursued further, but it should not distract us from a major conclusion to be drawn from Midili's studies. In stark contrast to those studies that have used traits from the Five-Factor Model or measures of general affect as their dispositional variables, these studies found substantial and replicable relations between personality measures and OCB. Further, studies of volunteerism provide additional evidence for an association between the prosocial personality orientation and planful, voluntary long-term prosocial actions.

In a study mentioned earlier, Penner and Finkelstein (1996) administered the PSB to a group of volunteers for an AIDS service organization and obtained information about their length of service for the organization. Five and 10 months later, the amount of time spent volunteering and the amount of contact the volunteers had, in a volunteer capacity, with someone who was HIV positive or had AIDS were also measured. Both dimensions of the PSB significantly correlated with length of service for the organization. Other-Oriented Empathy predicted the time spent volunteering 5 months after the PSB was administered; among male volunteers, Other-Oriented Empathy also predicted contact with someone with HIV/AIDS individuals 5 and 10 months later.

Why are these findings so different from what is typically found in studies of the personality correlates of prosocial behaviors in an organizational context? We believe that the major reason is that the characteristics measured in the PSB are more directly relevant to prosocial actions (including OCB) than are those measured by the Agreeableness dimension of the Big Five. That is, as suggested earlier, some (but certainly not all) workers engage in OCB simply because they are helpful people. Thus, if one wishes to predict this class of prosocial behaviors, one must measure personality characteristics that are directly related to prosocial thoughts, feelings, and actions. Agreeableness might appear to be such a characteristic (indeed, one of its facets is called Altruism), but other findings suggest that there may be more to a prosocial orientation than Agreeableness. For example, Penner et al. (1995) correlated the PSB dimensions with the Big Five factors. As one would expect, Other-Oriented Empathy correlates substantially with Agreeableness ($r > .50$). However, the other dimension of the prosocial personality, Helpfulness, which predicts OCB and several other prosocial behaviors, was essentially uncorrelated with Agreeableness. Thus, Agreeableness may not align very well with OCB; likewise, personality traits that are more specifically associated with prosocial actions may better predict OCB.

Of course, confidence in Midili's findings would be strengthened by independent replications of the results by other researchers, who used other measures of OCB in different organizational contexts. However, pending these replications, we would argue that Midili's data (along with those of McNeely & Meglino, 1994) suggest that it may be premature to write off personality factors as causes of OCB or to suggest that they only contribute to it indirectly through their influence on morale.

We must, however, be careful to place these results in the proper context. We are not proposing that the prosocial personality (or any other personality characteristic) is a better predictor of OCB than job satisfaction, mood, organizational justice, and other similar kinds of variables. Rather, we propose that prosocial dispositions may account for variability in OCB that cannot be explained by these variables. Also, we believe that even with the addition of personality variables there will still be substantial residual variance in predictions of OCB. One reason for this was suggested in the previous section. People probably engage in OCB for a wide variety of reasons and to satisfy a number of different needs. Some of these are directly related to prosocial personality orientations, others are not. Thus, if our goal is to explain as much variance in OCB as we can, then we should not exclude these other motives from our prediction models.

The next section of this article provides yet another reason for being cautious about the role individual difference variables play in OCB. Specifically, in many instances a full understanding of why people engage in OCB will require going beyond their personality and to consider how they perceive themselves and their roles in the organization. To explain this idea more fully and to introduce another possible cause of OCB, we will again begin with constructs and theories developed to understand volunteerism.

ROLE-IDENTITY THEORY AND VOLUNTEERISM

Piliavin and her colleagues (Callero, Howard, & Piliavin, 1987; Grube & Piliavin, 1996; Piliavin & Callero; 1991) proposed a sociological theory of the factors that sustain long-term volunteerism. Because research on volunteerism has it roots in traditional personality and social psychological approaches to prosocial actions, it is oriented toward understanding how personality characteristics, motives, social influence, and situational pressures affect the actions of individual volunteers. But as Grube and Piliavin (1996) pointed out, "volunteering ... is an habitual activity, performed within an organizational structure" (p. 2). Thus, they argue it would be a mistake to ignore the social structure in which this behavior occurs. This argument would also seem quite applicable to OCB.

Their theory of sustained volunteerism begins with organizational commitment, a construct familiar to OCB researchers. Grube and Piliavin (1996) proposed that positive organizational experiences among volunteers will increase their organizational commitment, but they used role-identity theory to explain how and why organizational commitment affects volunteer activities. Role-identity theory concerns the ways in which the roles people play (i.e., behaviors associated with a position) can affect the way they see themselves. It proposes that a role can become part of a person's personal identity or self-concept (Stryker, 1980). Thus, people can become linked to an organization through the internalization of the role they play within the organization; they may strive to maintain this role and the personal, professional, and social relationships associated with it.

Piliavin and her associates believe that in the case of volunteering, continued service in this role produces significant changes in a person's sense of self. Specifically, the role the volunteer plays within the organization becomes part of how the volunteer sees himself or herself. It is this role-identity that drives the volunteer's behavior because the role becomes internalized and the volunteer strives to make his or her behavior consonant with this role identity (Grube & Piliavin, 1996). Thus, the theory proposes that the effects of organizational commitment on volunteers' behavior may be mediated through a volunteer role-identity. That is, organizational commitment (or job attitudes) may cause a person to enact a volunteer role, and enacting this role creates a volunteer role-identity. But it is this role-identity that is the direct cause of the volunteer's actions.

Three separate studies of volunteerism have found results consistent with this model. Grube and Piliavin (1996) measured organizational commitment, role identity, and the number of hours worked among a group of cancer volunteers. They found a significant relation between organizational commitment and the number of hours spent volunteering. However when organizational commitment and a measure of a volunteer role identity were both entered into a hierarchical regression, the regression weight for organizational commitment became nonsignificant; whereas role identity explained significant amounts of unique variance in the number of hours worked. This indicates that role identity mediated the impact of organizational commitment on the volunteers' behavior (Baron & Kenny, 1986). Deaux and Stark (1996) measured the kinds of motives described earlier in this article and the role identity among volunteers working with a prison population. They found that the volunteers' motives were significantly related to the intention to volunteer, but this relation was also mediated by the volunteers' role identity. That is, the relation between motive and intention to volunteer became nonsignificant when role identity was entered into a regression equation with intention to volunteer as the criterion variable.

Finally, Penner and Finkelstein (1996) did not directly measure role identity, but their findings also strongly suggest that it mediated the impact of organizational commitment on the behavior of the AIDS volunteers they studied. They measured organizational commitment and amount of volunteer activities three times at 5-month intervals. They found that the initial assessment of the volunteers' organizational commitment predicted the volunteer activities 10 months later. However, when the intermediate, or 5-month, assessment of volunteer activities was entered into a regression equation, the regression weight for organizational commitment became nonsignificant. If one accepts the notion that volunteer activities at the time of the intermediate assessment was a valid indicator of role identity, then these results are quite consistent with those obtained by Grube and Piliavin and Deaux and Stark.

We believe that one can easily extrapolate from these findings to OCB. Specifically, we are suggesting that if workers consistently engage in OCB, they will come to see that as part of their role within the organization. Consequently, they may develop a personal identity that is consistent with this role. This is what Stryker (1980) called an "internalized positional designation" (p. 60). Further, because this role defines a person's relationship with the organization and individuals within the organization, employees who have internalized this role will strive to engage in behaviors that sustain it and the associated relationships. In other words, they will be good "organizational citizens." People within an organization will, of course, vary in the extent to which they adopt this role and the centrality of it to their self-concept.

A CONCEPTUAL MODEL OF THE CAUSES OF OCB

The research findings and theories reviewed lead to the conceptual model of the causes of long-term or enduring OCB presented in Figure 1. The model sees the development of enduring levels of OCB as a two-phase process. The first phase concerns the factors that predispose workers to engage in intermediate OCB; that is, a stable level of OCB that has been occurring for a relatively short period of time. The causes of intermediate OCB are the variables that have been discussed

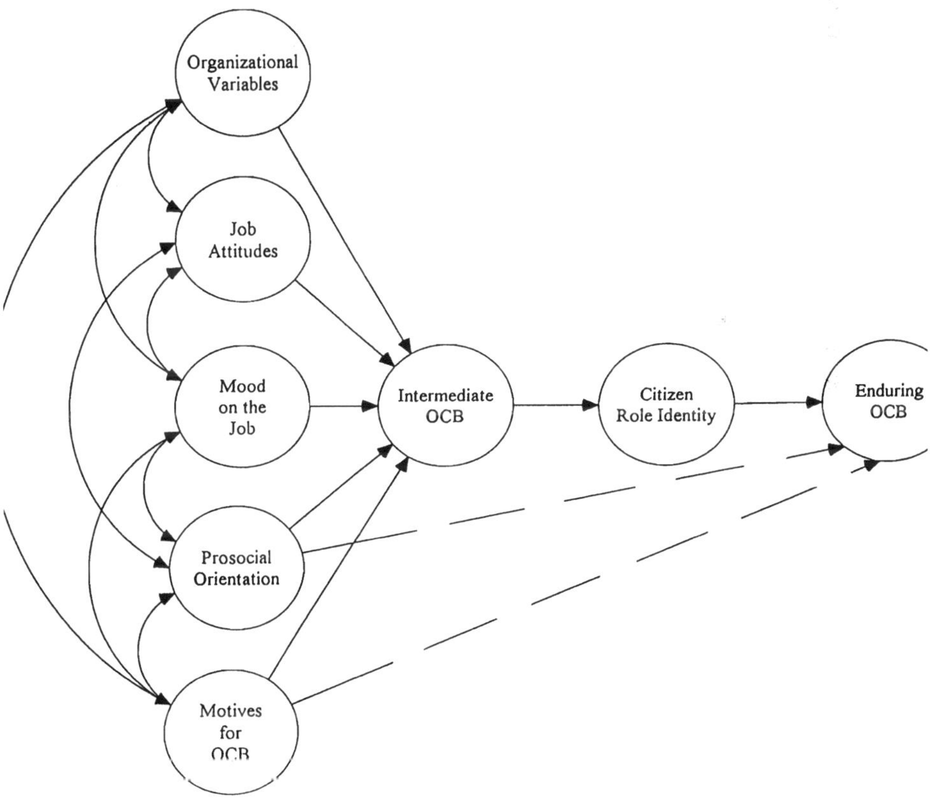

FIGURE 1 A conceptual model of the direct and indirect causes of organizational citizenship behavior (OCB). The dashed lines from Motives for OCB and Prosocial Orientation to Enduring OCB indicate that these variables also have a direct, but diminished impact on Enduring OCB.

in the previous sections of this article; they include job attitudes, organizational variables mood, motives, and personality characteristics, as well as other kinds of personal, demographic, and situational variables not specified in the model. The model posits that these causal variables are correlated with one another. Although it is not explicitly proposed in the model, it is certainly possible that some of these variables may be causally related to others. However, at this time, the model does not identify which, if any, of these relations are causal rather than correlational. Because this is only an initial version of the model, it also does not differentiate between the two major dimensions of OCB.

Role identity emerges in the second phase of the model. The model suggests that, over time, the direct impact of these variables on OCB diminishes. (However, it does not totally disappear; thus the dashed paths from Personality and Motives to Enduring OCB.) This is because the level of intermediate OCB affects the development of a role for a worker that concerns organizational citizenship. Those people who display high levels of OCB may begin to see this as one of their roles within the organization and to develop a personal and social identity that is consistent with this role. Part of their personal identity will be that of an organizational citizen. As a consequence, they engage in behaviors that will maintain this role and the relationships associated with it. It is the degree to which a person adopts a role identity of an "organizational citizen" that directly affects enduring OCB. That is, OCB covaries with the importance this role assumes in the person's self-concept and his or her relations with other people in the organization.[6]

Although all the individual paths in Figure 1 have been found in studies of OCB or volunteerism, at this time the total model is untested. But the constructs contained in it can all be translated into measurable variables and the viability of the model can be empirically determined through structural equation modeling or similar techniques. We believe that when this is done, the full model will be supported; however, empirical support for the model will not lead to the rejection of current knowledge about the causes of OCB. The model includes those variables that have been shown by prior research to cause OCB (e.g., job attitudes). However, it adds some important dispositional variables and suggests a link between psychological variables (e.g., attitudes, motives, and personality characteristics) and the more sociological causes of long-term OCB. Thus, the major consequence of a viable model of OCB that contains these new variables and relations should be a better understanding of what causes this phenomenon. And perhaps this understanding will provide us with the tools needed to increase the incidence of this important organizational behavior.

[6]Of course, as suggested earlier, not all people will engage in the same levels of intermediate OCB. And even among people who engage in similar levels of intermediate OCB, there will be both transient and stable differences in the importance of this behavior in people's role identity (because of things such as conflicting and competing roles).

REFERENCES

Adams, J. S. (1965). In equity in social exchange. In L. Berkowitz (Ed.), *Advances in experimental social psychology* (Vol. 2, pp. 267–299). New York: Academic.

Allen, K. (1982, Winter). Americans volunteer: 1981. *Voluntary Action Leadership*, 21–23.

Allen, T. D. (1996). *Examining the effects of performance beyond role requirements: A field and laboratory study*. Unpublished Doctoral Dissertation, University of Tennessee, Knoxville.

Baron, R. M., & Kenny, D. A. (1986). The moderator–mediator distinction in social psychological research: Conceptual, strategic, and statistical considerations. *Journal of Personality and Social Psychology, 51*, 1173–1182.

Borman, W. C., & Motowidlo, S. J. (1993). Expanding the criterion domain to include elements of contextual performance. In N. Schmitt & W. C. Borman (Eds.), *Personnel selection in organizations* (pp. 71–98). San Francisco: Jossey-Bass.

Borman, W. C., White, L. A., & Dorsey, D. W. (1995). Effects of ratee task performance and interpersonal factors on supervisor and peer performance ratings. *Journal of Applied Psychology, 80*, 168–177.

Callero, P. L., Howard, J. A., & Piliavin, J. A. (1987). Helping behavior as a role behavior: Disclosing social structure and history on the analysis of prosocial action. *Social Psychology Quarterly, 50*, 247–256.

Carlson, M., Charlin, V., & Miller, N. (1988). Positive mood and helping behavior: A test of six hypotheses. *Journal of Personality and Social Psychology, 55*, 211–229.

Cialdini, R. B. (1991). Altruism or egoism? That is still the question. *Psychological Inquiry, 2*, 124–126.

Clary, E. G., & Orenstein, L. (1991). The amount and effectiveness of help: The relationship of motives and abilities to helping behavior. *Personality and Social Psychology Bulletin, 17*, 58–64.

Clary, E. G., & Snyder, M. (1991). A functional analysis of altruism and prosocial behavior: The case of volunteerism. In M. S. Clark (Ed.), *Review of personality and social psychology: Vol. 12. Prosocial behavior* (pp. 119–148). Knobbier Park, CA: Sage.

Clary, E. G., Snyder, M., Ridge, R., Copeland, J., Haugen, J., & Miene, P. (1996). *Understanding the motivations of volunteers: A functional approach*. Unpublished manuscript, College of St. Catherine, St. Paul, MN.

Clary, E. G., Snyder, M., Ridge, R., Miene, P., & Haugen, J. (1994). Matching messages to motives in persuasion: A functional approach to promoting volunteerism. *Journal of Applied Social Psychology, 24*, 1129–1149.

Cook, T. D., & Campbell, D. T. (1979). *Quasi-experimentation design and analysis issues for field settings*. Boston: Houghton Mifflin.

Costa, P. T., & McCrae, R. R. (1992). *NEO-PI-R professional manual*. Odessa, FL: Psychological Assessment Resources.

Davis, M. H. (1980). A multidimensional approach to individual differences in empathy. *JSAS Catalog of Selected Documents in Psychology, 10*, 85.

Deaux, K., & Stark, B. E. (1996). *Identity and motive: An integrated theory of volunteerism*. Ann Arbor, MI: Society for the Psychological Study of Social Issues.

Dovidio, J. F., Piliavin, J. A., Gaertner, S. L., Schroeder, D. A., & Clark, R. D., III (1991). The arousal: Cost-reward model and the process of intervention: A review of the evidence. In M. S. Clark (Ed.), *Review of personality and social psychology: Vol. 12. Prosocial behavior* (pp. 86–118). Newbury Park, CA: Sage.

Eagly, A. H., & Chaiken, S. (1993). *The psychology of attitudes*. Forth Worth, TX: Harcourt Brace Jovanovich.

Funder, D. C. (1994). Two cheers for the big five! *Psychological Inquiry, 5*, 125–127.

George, J. M. (1991). State or trait: The effects of positive mood on prosocial behaviors at work. *Journal of Applied Psychology, 76*, 299–307.

George, J. M., & Brief, A. P. (1992). Feeling good—doing good: A conceptual analysis of the mood at work-organizational spontaneity relationship. *Psychological Bulletin, 112,* 310–329.

Gilligan, C. (1982). *In a different voice: Psychological theory and women's development.* Cambridge, MA: Harvard University Press.

Grube, J. A., & Piliavin, J. A. (1996, May). *Role identity, organizational commitment, and volunteer performance.* Paper presented at the Meeting of the Society for the Psychological Study of Social Issues, Ann Arbor, MI.

Hanson, M. A. (1991). *Volunteer motivation.* Unpublished paper, University of Minnesota, Minneapolis.

Isen, A. (1993). Positive affect and decision making. In M. Lewis & M. Haviland (Eds.), *Handbook of emotion* (pp. 261–267). New York: Guilford.

Isen, A., Clark, M., & Schwartz, M. F. (1976). Duration of the effect of good mood on helping: "Footprints on the sands of time." *Journal of Personality and Social Psychology, 34,* 385–393.

Latané, B., & Darley, J. M. (1970). *The unresponsive bystander: Why doesn't he help?* New York: Appleton-Century-Crofts.

McNeely, B. L., & Meglino, B. M. (1994). The role of dispositional and situational antecedents of prosocial organizational behavior: An examination of the intended beneficiaries or prosocial behavior. *Journal of Applied Psychology, 79,* 836–844.

Midili, A. R. (1995). Unpublished doctoral dissertation, University of South Florida, Tampa.

Midili, A. R. & Penner, L. A. (1995, August). *Dispositional and environmental influences on Organizational Citizenship Behavior.* Paper presented at the meeting of the American Psychological Association, New York.

Motowidlo, S. J., & Van Scotter, J. R. (1994). Evidence that task performance should be distinguished from contextual performance. *Journal of Applied Psychology, 79,* 475–480.

Omoto, A., & Snyder, M. (1995). Sustained helping without obligation: Motivation, longevity of service, and perceived attitude change among AIDS volunteers. *Journal of Personality and Social Psychology, 68,* 671–687.

Omoto, A. M., Snyder, M., & Berghuis, J. P. (1993). The psychology of volunteerism: A conceptual analysis and a program of action research. In J. B. Pryor & G. Reeder (Eds.), *The social psychology of HIV infection* (pp. 333–356). Hillsdale, NJ: Lawrence Erlbaum Associates, Inc.

Organ, D. W. (1988). *Organizational citizenship behavior: The good soldier syndrome.* Lexington, MA: Lexington.

Organ, D. W. (1990). The motivational basis of organizational citizenship behavior. In B. M. Staw & L. L. Cummings (Eds.), *Research in organizational behavior* (Vol. 1, pp. 43–72). Greenwich, CT: JAI.

Organ, D. W. (1993, March). *Personality and organization citizenship behavior: A not-very-encouraging scorecard so far.* Paper presented at the meeting of the Society for Industrial and Organizational Psychology, San Francisco.

Organ, D. W., & Konovsky, M. (1989). Cognitive versus affective determinants of organizational citizenship behavior. *Journal of Applied Psychology, 74,* 157–164.

Organ, D. W., & Ryan, K. (1995). A meta-analytic review of attitudinal and dispositional predictors of organizational citizenship behavior. *Personnel Psychology, 48,* 775–802.

Penner, L. A., & Craiger, J. P. (1991, August). *The altruistic personality: A case of multiple identities?* Paper presented at the meeting of the American Psychological Association, San Francisco, CA.

Penner, L. A. & Finkelstein, M. (1996, May). *Prosocial personality orientations and volunteerism.* Paper presented at the meeting of the Society for the Psychological Study of Social Issues, Ann Arbor, MI.

Penner, L. A., Fritzsche, B. A., Craiger, J. P., & Freifeld, T. R. (1995). Measuring the prosocial personality. In J. Butcher & C. D. Spielberger (Eds.), *Advances in personality assessment* (Vol. 10, pp.147–163). Hillsdale, NJ: Lawrence Erlbaum Associates, Inc.

Piliavin, J. A., & Callero, P. (1991). *Giving blood: The development of an altruistic identity*. Baltimore: Johns Hopkins University Press.

Podsakoff, P. M., & MacKenzie, S. B. (1989). *A second generation measure of organizational citizenship behavior*. Unpublished manuscript, Indiana University.

Rushton, J. P., Chrisjohn, R. D., & Fekken, G. C. (1981). The altruistic personality and the self-report altruism scale. *Personality and Individual Differences, 2,* 293–302.

Schroeder, D. A., Penner, L. A., Dovidio, J. F., & Piliavin, J. A. (1995). *The psychology of helping and altruism.* New York: McGraw-Hill.

Schwartz, S. H., & Howard, J. (1982). A normative decision-making model of helping behavior. In J. P. Rushton & R. M. Sorrentino (Eds.), *Altruism and helping behavior* (pp. 189–211). Hillsdale, NJ: Lawrence Erlbaum Associates, Inc.

Skarlicki, D. P., & Latham, G. P. (1996). Increasing citizenship behavior within a labor union: A test of organizational justice theory. *Journal of Applied Psychology, 81,* 161–169.

Smith, C. A., Organ, D. W., & Near, J. P. (1983). Organizational citizenship behavior: Its nature and antecedents. *Journal of Applied Psychology, 68,* 653–663.

Snyder, M. (1993). Basic research and practical problems: The promise of a functional personality and social psychology. *Personality and Social Psychology Bulletin, 19,* 251–264.

Stryker, S. (1980). *Symbolic interactionism.* Menlo Park, CA: Benjamin/Cummings.

Thibaut, J., & Kelley, H. (1959). *The social psychology of groups.* New York: Wiley.

Walster, E., Walster, G. W., & Berscheid, E. (1978). *Equity: Theory and research.* Boston: Allyn & Bacon.

Watson, D., & Clarke, L. A. (1992). Negative affectivity: The disposition to experience aversive emotional states. *Psychological Bulletin, 96,* 465–490.

Wright, C. (1996). *An examination of the influence of mood, procedural justice and prosocial personality on organizational citizenship behavior.* Unpublished dissertation, University of South Florida, Tampa.

HUMAN PERFORMANCE, *10*(2), 133–151

Impact of Organizational Citizenship Behavior on Organizational Performance: A Review and Suggestions for Future Research

Philip M. Podsakoff
Department of Management
Indiana University

Scott B. MacKenzie
Department of Marketing
Indiana University

Despite the widespread interest in the topic of organizational citizenship behaviors (OCBs), little empirical research has tested the fundamental assumption that these forms of behavior improve the effectiveness of work groups or organizations. This article examines the assumption that OCBs improve the effectiveness of work groups or organizations in which they are exhibited. First, several theoretical/conceptual explanations of why OCBs may improve organizational effectiveness are provided. Following this, a review of the available empirical evidence is provided. The results of this review indicate that OCBs make important contributions to the variance in organizational effectiveness, although helping behavior tends to have more systematic effects than either sportsmanship or civic virtue. Finally, the implications of these findings for future research are discussed.

One of the most widely studied topics in organizational behavior research in recent years is organizational citizenship behaviors (OCBs; cf. Bateman & Organ, 1983; Borman & Motowidlo, 1993; Brief & Motowidlo, 1986; George & Bettenhausen, 1990; Moorman, 1991; Munene, 1995; Niehoff & Moorman, 1993; Organ, 1988,

Requests for reprints should be sent to Philip M. Podsakoff, Department of Management, School of Business, Indiana University, Bloomington, IN 47405. E-mail: podsakof@indiana.edu

1990; Organ & Konovsky, 1989; Organ & Ryan, 1995; Podsakoff, MacKenzie, & Bommer, 1996a, 1996b; Podsakoff, MacKenzie, & Fetter, 1993; Podsakoff, MacKenzie, Moorman, & Fetter, 1990; Puffer, 1987; Skarlicki & Latham, 1996; Smith, Organ, & Near, 1983; Williams & Anderson, 1991). Although a number of conceptually distinct dimensions of OCBs have been identified (Organ, 1988, 1990), including altruism, courtesy, cheerleading, peacekeeping, sportsmanship, civic virtue, and conscientiousness, recent empirical research (cf. MacKenzie, Podsakoff, & Fetter, 1991, 1993; Podsakoff & MacKenzie, 1994) indicates that managers often have difficulty recognizing some of these fine distinctions and tend to lump altruism, courtesy, cheerleading, and peacekeeping into a single "helping" behavior dimension. Conceptually, helping behavior is a second-order latent construct, consisting of Organ's (1988, 1990) altruism, courtesy, peacekeeping, and some aspects of his cheerleading dimensions. The first three of these dimensions clearly involve helping others with, or preventing the occurrence of, work-related problems. In addition, cheerleading can also be viewed as helping behavior when an employee encourages a coworker who is discouraged about his or her accomplishments or professional development. Thus, all four of these forms of citizenship involve aspects of helping behavior.

The widespread interest in organizational citizenship stems primarily from the belief that these behaviors enhance organizational effectiveness. Because of this, a great deal of research (cf. Ball, Trevino, & Sims, 1994; Bateman & Organ, 1983; Brief & Motowidlo, 1986; Farh, Podsakoff, & Organ, 1990; George, 1990; George & Bettenhausen, 1990; Moorman, 1991; Munene, 1995; Niehoff & Moorman, 1993; Organ & Konovsky, 1989; Organ & Ryan, 1995; Podsakoff et al., 1996a, 1996b; Podsakoff et al., 1993; Podsakoff et al., 1990; Podsakoff, Niehoff, MacKenzie, & Williams, 1993; Puffer, 1987; Schnake, 1991; Smith et al., 1983; Williams & Anderson, 1991) has attempted to identify those subordinate characteristics (e.g., conscientiousness, agreeableness, positive and negative affectivity, etc.), task characteristics (task scope, task feedback, intrinsically satisfying tasks, etc.), organizational characteristics (e.g., formalization, inflexibility, spatial distance, etc.), and/or leader behaviors (e.g., leader supportiveness, contingent reward behavior, transformational leadership behaviors, etc.) that encourage employees to exhibit OCBs. In view of all of this activity, it is therefore surprising that more research has not attempted to empirically test whether OCBs really do influence organizational effectiveness. Indeed, as noted by Organ and Konovsky (1989),

> OCB derives its practical importance from the premise that it represents contributions that do not inhere in formal role obligations. The presumption is that many of these contributions, aggregated over time and persons, enhance organizational effectiveness. [However], this presumption rests more on its plausibility than direct empirical support. (p. 157)

Similarly, Borman and Motowidlo (1993) noted that the "link between organizational effectiveness and performance ... [is] typically logical and conceptual rather than empirical" (p. 88). Within this context, the purpose of this article is to examine the relation between OCB and organizational effectiveness. First, several theoretical/conceptual explanations of why OCBs might influence organizational or work group effectiveness are explored. Following this, the empirical evidence of the effects of OCBs on organizational and work group performance is reviewed. Finally, the article closes with a discussion of the implications of these findings and suggestions for future research.

REASONS FOR THE IMPACT OF OCBs ON WORK GROUP AND ORGANIZATIONAL EFFECTIVENESS

There are several possible reasons why helping, sportsmanship, and civic virtue might be positively related to work group or organizational effectiveness (cf. Borman & Motowidlo, 1993; George & Bettenhausen, 1991; Karambayya, 1990; MacKenzie et al., 1991, 1993; Organ, 1988, 1990; Podsakoff & MacKenzie, 1994; Podsakoff, MacKenzie, & Hui, 1993; Smith et al., 1983). In general, it has been argued (cf. Borman & Motowidlo, 1993; Organ, 1988; Smith et al., 1983) that citizenship behaviors may enhance performance by "lubricating" the social machinery of the organization, reducing friction, and/or increasing efficiency. Table 1 summarizes some of the ways in which this may happen.

One way that OCBs may increase the efficiency of an organization is by enhancing coworker or managerial productivity (cf. MacKenzie et al., 1991, 1993; Organ, 1988; Podsakoff & MacKenzie, 1994). For example, when more experienced employees voluntarily help new coworkers "learn the ropes," it helps the new workers to become productive employees faster, thus enhancing the efficiency of the work group or unit. Similarly, over time, helping behavior can be the mechanism through which "best practices" are spread throughout a work unit or group. Managerial productivity may also increase when employees (a) provide valuable suggestions for improving unit performance or feedback on his or her ideas (civic virtue) and (b) avoid creating problems for coworkers (courtesy), which allows the manager to escape the trap of falling into a pattern of "crisis" management.

Another way that OCBs may enhance the efficiency of an organization is by freeing up various types of resources for more productive purposes (cf. Borman & Motowidlo, 1993; MacKenzie et al., 1991, 1993; Organ, 1988; Podsakoff et al., 1993). For example, employees who help each other with work-related problems allow the manager to spend more time on productive tasks (e.g., strategic planning, improving business processes, securing valuable resources, etc.). Likewise, when employees are conscientious it frees up a manager's time because the manager can delegate more responsibility to them and they require less supervision. In a similar

TABLE 1
Summary of Reasons Why OCBs Might Influence Organizational Effectiveness

Potential Reasons Why OCBs Influence Work Group and/or Organizational Performance	*Examples*
OCBs may enhance coworker productivity	• Employees who help another coworker "learn the ropes" may help them to become more productive employees faster. • Over time, helping behavior can help to spread "best practices" throughout the work unit or group.
OCBs may enhance managerial productivity	• If employees engage in civic virtue, the manager may receive valuable suggestions and/or feedback on his or her ideas for improving unit effectiveness. • Courteous employees, who avoid creating problems for coworkers, allow the manager to avoid falling into a pattern of "crisis" management.
OCBs may free resources up for more productive purposes	• If employees help each other with work-related problems, then the manager doesn't have too; consequently, the manager can spend more time on productive tasks, such as planning. • Employees that exhibit conscientiousness require less managerial supervision and permit the manager to delegate more responsibility to them. • To the extent that experienced employees help in the training and orienting of new employees, it reduces the need to devote organizational resources to these activities. • If employees exhibit sportsmanship, it frees the manager from having to spend too much of his or her time dealing with petty complaints.
OCBs may reduce the need to devote scarce resources to purely maintenance functions	• A natural by-product of helping behavior is that it enhances team spirit, morale, and cohesiveness, thus reducing the need for group members (or managers) to spend energy and time on group maintenance functions. • Employees that exhibit courtesy toward others reduce intergroup conflict; thereby diminishing the time spent on conflict management activities.
OCBs may serve as an effective means of coordinating activities between team members and across work groups	• Exhibiting civic virtue by voluntarily attending and actively participating in work unit meetings would help the coordination of effort among team members, thus potentially increasing the group's effectiveness and efficiency. • Exhibiting courtesy by "touching base" with other team members or members of other functional groups in the organization reduces the likelihood of the occurrence of problems that would otherwise take time and effort to resolve.

TABLE 1 (Continued)

Potential Reasons Why OCBs Influence Work Group and/or Organizational Performance	*Examples*
OCBs may enhance the organization's ability to attract and retain the best people by making it a more attractive place to work	• Helping behaviors may enhance morale, group cohesiveness, and the sense of belonging to a team, all of which may enhance performance and help the organization to attract and retain better employees. • Demonstrating sportsmanship by being willing to "roll with the punches" and not complaining about trivial matters sets an example for others, and thereby develops a sense of loyalty and commitment to the organization that may enhance employee retention.
OCBs may enhance the stability of organizational performance	• Picking up the slack for others that are absent, or who have heavy workloads, can help to enhance the stability (reduce the variability) of the work unit's performance. • Conscientious employees are more likely to maintain a consistently high level of output, thus reducing variability in a work unit's performance.
OCBs may enhance an organization's ability to adapt to environmental changes	• Employees who are in close contact with the marketplace volunteer information about changes in the environment and make suggestions about how to respond to them; it helps an organization to adapt. • Employees who attend and actively participate in meetings may aid the dissemination of information in an organization, thus enhancing its responsiveness. • Employees who exhibit sportsmanship, by demonstrating a willingness to take on new responsibilities or learn new skills, enhance the organization's ability to adapt to changes in its environment.

Note. OCB = organizational citizenship behavior.

manner, when employees exhibit sportsmanship, a manager's time is not wasted dealing with petty complaints. Perhaps more generally, and to the extent that experienced employees help in the training and orienting of new employees, it reduces the resources the organization must devote to these activities.

Citizenship behaviors may also improve organizational performance by (a) reducing the need to devote scarce resources to purely maintenance functions (Organ, 1988) and (b) helping to coordinate the activities of work groups (cf. Karambayya, 1990; Smith ct al., 1983). A natural by-product of hclping bchavior is that it enhances team spirit, morale, and cohesiveness, thus reducing the need for group members (or managers) to spend energy and time on group maintenance functions. Likewise, not creating problems for others (exhibiting courtesy) reduces intergroup conflict and diminishes the need to spend time on conflict management activities. The coordination of activities among group members and between work groups may also be enhanced when employees voluntarily attend and actively participate in work unit meetings (civic virtue) and/or "touch base" with other team members or members of other groups to avoid creating problems for them (courtesy).

OCB may also improve performance by enhancing the organization's ability to attract and retain the best people (cf. George & Bettenhausen, 1990; Organ, 1988). Many of the best employees and job candidates enjoy working in a positive environment with a closely knit group of coworkers. Helping behaviors may directly contribute to such an environment by enhancing morale and fostering group cohesiveness and a sense of belonging to a team, thus making the organization a more attractive place to work. Related to this, when employees exhibit sportsmanship by being willing to "roll with the punches," and refrain from complaining about trivial matters, it sets an example of putting the interests of the work unit or group ahead of one's own interests; thus enhancing a sense of loyalty and commitment to the organization.

It is also possible that OCBs benefit an organization by reducing the variability in its performance. Minimizing variability is important because it allows managers to more easily plan and allocate scarce resources. There are several things employees may do to reduce the variability in a work unit's performance, including voluntary acts such as (a) picking up the slack for others that are absent or who have heavy workloads (helping), (b) coming in early or staying late to finish important projects (conscientiousness), and/or (c) going "above and beyond the call of duty" in performing one's work responsibilities (conscientiousness). Individually, these behaviors may all be trivial, but collectively they may significantly enhance the performance of an organization.

Finally, OCBs may help to enhance an organization's ability to adapt to changing environments in several ways. For example, when employees who are in close contact with the marketplace volunteer information about changes in the environment and make suggestions about how to respond to them, it helps an organization to adapt. Similarly, when employees voluntarily attend and actively participate in meetings (civic virtue), it may enhance an organization's responsiveness by aiding the dissemination of valuable information. In addition, when employees exhibit sportsmanship by demonstrating a willingness to take on new responsibilities or learn new skills, it may enhance an organization's ability to adapt to changes in its environment.

Thus, OCBs may contribute to organizational success by (a) enhancing coworker and managerial productivity, (b) freeing up resources so they can be used for more productive purposes, (c) reducing the need to devote scarce resources to purely maintenance functions, (d) helping to coordinate the activities both within and across work groups, (e) strengthening the organization's ability to attract and retain the best employees, (f) increasing the stability of the organization's performance, and (g) enabling the organization to more effectively adapt to environmental changes.

EVIDENCE OF THE EFFECTS OF OCBs ON WORK GROUP AND ORGANIZATIONAL SUCCESS

The assumption that OCBs contribute to the effectiveness of work teams and organizations has only recently been tested empirically. Perhaps the first person to explore this issue was Karambayya (1990), who examined the relation between work unit performance and satisfaction and unit members' citizenship behaviors in a sample of 18 intact work groups, comprised primarily of white-collar and professional employees from 12 different organizations. In her study, she obtained performance ratings for the work units from key division and department heads, employee OCB ratings from supervisors, and self-reports of satisfaction from employees. Consistent with her expectations, she found that employees in high-performing work units were more satisfied and exhibited more citizenship behaviors than employees in low-performing work units.

However, despite Karambayya's (1990) relatively encouraging findings, there are some limitations to her study. First, Karambayya's (1990) measures were subjective ratings provided by key informants in each of 12 different organizations, rather than quantitative indices of work unit or organizational success. Thus, although she observed a relation between OCBs and subjective ratings of unit performance, the question of whether OCBs influence objective unit performance remains unanswered. For example, the strength of the relation between citizenship behavior and performance may be influenced by the key informants' implicit theories (cf. Berman & Kenny, 1976; Bruner & Tagiuri, 1954) of the relation between these two constructs. Second, because Karambayya had different raters evaluating performance in each of the 12 organizations in her sample, we do not know whether the measurement metric used by all of the raters was the same. Because it is likely that the organizations differed in their products, services, corporate cultures, and standards, it seems questionable that the same measurement metric would have been used by all raters. Third, as noted by Bagozzi, Yi, and Phillips (1991), measurement error can sometimes be quite high in key informant reports. Finally, although Karambayya (1990) identified two groups of work units and labelled 11 of them as "high" and 7 of them as "low" performing units, there is really no assurance that the two groups did not differ on other factors as well. Thus, although Karambayya's (1990) results were promising, they were far from conclusive.

A series of recent studies (cf. Podsakoff, Ahearne, & MacKenzie, in press; Podsakoff & MacKenzie, 1994; MacKenzie, Podsakoff, & Ahearne, 1996; Walz & Niehoff, 1996) addressed many of the limitations of Karambayya's research.

Unlike Karambayya's study, these studies all used objective measures of unit performance and held variations due to industry factors constant by sampling multiple units within the same company. Thus, any observed relations between citizenship behavior and performance are less likely to be affected by implicit theories, different measurement metrics, or measurement error. In addition, there was a great deal of consistency in the manner in which OCBs were measured across the studies, thus making it easier to compare their results.

A summary of these four studies is provided in Table 2. As indicated in this table, four different organizational contexts have been examined. Podsakoff and MacKenzie (1994) examined 116 insurance agency units, Podsakoff et al. (in press) examined 40 paper mill work crews, MacKenzie et al. (1996) examined 306 pharmaceutical sales teams, and Walz and Niehoff (1996) examined 30 limited-menu restaurants. In addition, aspects of both the quantity and quality of performance were examined in these studies.

In the first study, Podsakoff and MacKenzie (1994) examined the impact of helping behavior, sportsmanship, and civic virtue on a composite index of unit performance. This composite index was developed by the company for the purpose of assessing unit success, and was the index on which units compete for sales incentives (i.e., awards, trips, prizes, etc.). This index was comprised of a weighted average of four measures, including the (a) amount of "new business" brought in by the agents, (b) amount the agents exceeded the previous year's median agent production level for the company, (c) average number of policies sold per agent weeks worked, and (d) total number of polices sold by the agents. Podsakoff and MacKenzie found that all three forms of citizenship behaviors had significant effects on unit-level performance, and together accounted for approximately 17% of the variance. However, contrary to their expectations, they found that helping behavior was negatively (rather than positively) related to unit performance.

In the second study, Podsakoff et al. (in press) examined the effects of helping behavior, sportsmanship, and civic virtue on both the quantity and quality of the paper produced by 40 work crews at a paper mill. Compensation for each crew member was based on a combination of hourly wages and gain-sharing based on the quantity and quality of the paper that each crew produced. Podsakoff et al. (1996) found that helping behavior and sportsmanship were positively related to the quantity of paper produced, and that helping behavior reduced the percentage of paper rejected, which means that it was positively related to production quality. These predictors accounted for nearly 26% of the variance in production quantity, and almost 17% in production quality.

In the third study, MacKenzie et al. (1996) examined the effects of helping behavior, sportsmanship, and civic virtue on the effectiveness of 306 pharmaceutical sales teams. The teams were responsible for marketing four product lines directly to physicians, as opposed to managed-care, government organizations, or hospitals. Members of the sales teams were compensated based on the team's

TABLE 2
Summary of Results Across Studies

	Podsakoff & MacKenzie (1994)[a]	*Podsakoff et al. (1996)*[b]		*MacKenzie et al. (1996)*[c]	*Walz & Niehoff (1996)*[d]					
Description	*Index of Sales Performance*	*Quantity Produced*[e]	*Product Quality*[f]	*% of Team Sales Quota*	*Food Cost %*	*Revenue FTE*	*Operating Efficiency*	*Customer Complaints*	*Customer Satisfaction*	*Quality of Performance*
Helping Behavior → Organizational Performance	−.494*	.397*	−.424*	.18*	−.46*	4581.6*	3.56*	—	.42***	.13*
Civic Virtue → Organizational Performance	.529*	−.318	.044	.18*	—	—	—	−.76**	—	—
Sportsmanship → Organizational Performance	.325*	.393*	−.028	.07	−.29*	—	—	.47+	—	—
R^2	17%	25.7%	16.7%	15%	43%	18%	15%	37%	39%	20%

Note. With the exception of Walz and Niehoff (1996), coefficients reported are standardized parameter estimates.
[a]N = 116 insurance agency units. [b]N = 40 paper mill work crews. [c]N = 306 pharmaceutical sales teams. [d]N = 30 limited-menu restaurants. [e]Percentage of maximum production. [f]Percentage of paper rejected.
$*p < .05$. $**p < .01$. $***p < .001$. $+p < .06$.

overall performance, rather than on the basis of their individual performance. As indicated in Table 2, MacKenzie et al. found that both helping behavior and sportsmanship were positively related to sales team effectiveness, and together accounted for accounted for approximately 15% of the variance in this criterion variable.

In the final study, Walz and Niehoff (1996) tested the relations between OCBs and a variety of performance measures in limited-menu restaurants. They measured OCBs using slightly modified versions of MacKenzie et al.'s (1993) and Podsakoff and MacKenzie's (1994) OCB scales. They found that helping behavior was related to overall operating efficiency, revenue to full-time-equivalent, customer satisfaction, and quality of performance, in addition to reduced food cost percentage (which represents the percentage of food and ingredients wasted). Sportsmanship was negatively associated with the percentage of wasted food and customer complaints. Civic virtue correlated negatively with the number of customer complaints. Overall, one of the most impressive aspects of their findings is that the combination of helping, sportsmanship, and civic virtue accounted for an average of about 29% of the variance in these six objective criterion variables, with the proportion of variance accounted for as high as 37% to 43% for some of these variables.

Taken together, the overall pattern of results provide general support for the hypothesis that OCBs are related to organizational effectiveness. Across four diverse samples, OCBs accounted for an average of approximately 19% of the variance in performance quantity, over 18% of the variance in the quality of performance, about 25% of the variance in financial efficiency indicators (operating efficiency, food cost percentage, and revenue full-time-equivalent), and about 38% of the variance in customer service indicators (customer satisfaction and customer complaints). Helping behavior had significant effects on every indicator of performance, except customer complaints in the Walz and Niehoff (1996) study. Generally speaking, helping behavior was found to enhance performance. The only exception was that helping behavior had a negative impact on the quantity of performance in the sample of insurance agency units examined by Podsakoff and MacKenzie (1994). Sportsmanship had more limited effects. It enhanced the quantity of performance in two of the three samples where it was studied (insurance agency units and paper mill work crews) and increased some aspects of financial efficiency and customer service in the limited-menu restaurant sample. Finally, civic virtue was found to enhance the quantity of performance in the insurance and pharmaceutical sales samples and to reduce customer complaints in the limited-menu restaurant sample. Thus, the available empirical research clearly supports Organ's (1988) fundamental assumption that OCB is related to performance—although the evidence is stronger for some forms of citizenship behavior (i.e., helping) than for others (i.e., sportsmanship and civic virtue).

IMPLICATIONS FOR FUTURE RESEARCH

In view of the fact that OCBs have been found to be related to organizational effectiveness, there are a number of important issues future research should address. Four major types of issues are discussed in the following sections: potential moderators of the relation between OCBs and unit effectiveness, the need to more accurately assess the direction of causality between OCBs and organizational success, the need to examine additional forms of extra-role behavior, and the need to broaden the measures of organizational performance examined.

Potential Moderators of the OCB–Quantity of Performance Relation

Two interesting aspects of the empirical findings shown in Table 2 are that (a) helping behavior sometimes increased, and sometimes decreased, the quantity of performance and (b) sportsmanship and civic virtue seem to have had an impact on this criterion variable in some samples, but not in others. This suggests that there may be factors that moderate the impact of OCBs on the quantity of performance.

There are a number of potential reasons why the relation between helping behavior and the quantity of performance was negative in one sample (Podsakoff & MacKenzie, 1994) and positive in the others (MacKenzie et al., 1996; Podsakoff et al., in press). One relates to the nature of the samples in the three studies. For example, in the life insurance sample studied by Podsakoff and MacKenzie (1994), turnover was extremely high (45% in their first year of employment and over 80% within the first 5 years) and the average tenure of the agents with the company was only 5.29 years. This led Podsakoff and MacKenzie (1994) to speculate that although inexperienced agents may sell more with the help of experienced agents, many of the inexperienced agents may not stay with the company very long. Thus, the increase in their sales productivity resulting from the help they receive from the experienced agents may not offset the corresponding decrease in the experienced agents' sales caused by their taking time out to help inexperienced agents. In contrast, the average tenure of the crew members in the sample of paper mill employees studied by Podsakoff et al. (in press) was over 18 years, and the average tenure among the pharmaceutical sales people studied by MacKenzie et al. (1996) was also quite long. As a result, it is likely that helping behavior provided by crew members or pharmaceutical sales team members actually paid off in terms of increased productivity.

Another potential reason for the differences in the findings relates to the compensation systems in the three samples. In the insurance sales sample, agents were compensated on the basis of their individual sales performance. Indeed, no part of their pay was related to their agency's performance. Under such individualistic compensation systems, agents might be less willing to provide help to their peers, or might be less concerned with the quality of their suggestions, because there are no personal consequences for them. On the other hand, in the pharmaceutical sales sample, compensation was completely determined by team performance, and in the sample of paper mill work crews, compensation was based partially on team performance and partially on the basis of job responsibilities and tenure. Thus, one could argue that when a portion of one's pay is determined by group effort, OCBs might be expected to be directed at helping and supporting one's peers.

Still another potential moderator of the helping behavior → quantity of performance relation is the technological requirements of the job. For example, Organ (1988) noted that,

> Using Thompson's (1967) taxonomy, one would expect OCB to have more importance in connection with intensive than with mediating or long-linked technologies, because intensive technologies give rise to mutual dependence among members and require spontaneous give-and-take, accommodating gestures among the parties in order to achieve effective coordination of their respective efforts. (p. 109)

Similarly, one would expect OCBs to be more critical to organizational and work group success when long-linked technologies, as opposed to mediating technologies, are employed. Unlike the mediating technologies employed in the insurance industry, which require virtually no cooperative effort or mutual dependence among the agents, the long-linked technologies used in the paper industry require what Thompson (1967) called serial interdependence among the crew members. This type of interdependence demands a considerable amount of joint or cooperative effort by the work group to accomplish the task. Thus, differences in the relation obtained between helping behavior and work unit performance in the two studies may, in part, reflect differences in the nature of the dependency relations required in the two different types of jobs included in the two studies.

In addition to the potential moderators of the relation between helping behavior and the quantity of performance, the results suggest that there may also be some potential moderators of the relation between civic virtue and the quantity of performance. Table 2 shows that civic virtue had a positive impact on performance for the two sales samples, but not for the paper mill sample. At the risk of overinterpreting the findings of only three studies, it is possible that this pattern of findings results from the nature of the job included in the samples. Sales people are boundary spanners, who are one of the primary points of contact between a company and its customers, competitors, and the environment in general. As such, they often possess information regarding customers, the competitive environment, and/or business trends that others in the organization do not possess, and which may be critical for allowing the organization to adapt to changes in its environment. Thus, to the extent that salespeople actively participate in meetings, provide constructive suggestions about how to improve the way in which the organization does its business, and are willing to risk disapproval to express their beliefs about what is best for the organization, they may enhance the organization's performance. Future research should explore this possibility in greater detail.

Another possibility noted by Podsakoff et al. (in press) is that the differential impact of civic virtue on the quantity of performance across the settings may be a result of the differential quality of suggestions or the nature of participation by work group members. It is possible that suggestions are not helpful or that participation does not result in useful discourse for some organizations. In such cases, high civic virtue would not translate into high organizational effectiveness.

Taken together, the previous discussion suggests that future research examining the relation between OCBs and organizational effectiveness could benefit from examining the moderating effects of organizational characteristics (i.e., the level of turnover, the nature of the compensation system, etc.) and task and technological requirements (i.e., the nature of the technology and/or tasks that employees perform, the amount of team work required across jobs, etc.). In addition, future research might also investigate the potential moderating effects of individual differences such as ability, experience, training, and knowledge. It seems plausible that an OCB like helping behavior might have different effects on performance in units where employees are low in ability, experience, training, or knowledge than in units where employees have high levels of ability, experience, training, or knowledge.

Investigation of Causality

Another important topic for future research to investigate is the question of whether (a) OCBs cause organizational performance, (b) organizational performance causes OCBs, or (c) the relation between OCBs and performance is spurious due to a common cause (the third variable). Although throughout this article, and indeed throughout all OCB research, the fundamental assumption is that OCBs cause unit effectiveness, there has never been a direct test of this assumption. All of the evidence summarized in this article is correlational in nature, and thus is not capable of clearly distinguishing the direction of causality. For example, the positive relations observed between OCBs and unit performance have been interpreted as an indication that OCBs cause performance to increase. However, it is also possible that units that perform well have more time, are under less pressure, and/or have members who are more satisfied than units that are not performing well; therefore they are more willing to engage in extra-role behaviors like helping, sportsmanship, and civic virtue. This suggests it is a unit's level of performance that causes citizenship behavior rather than vice versa. Or, it is possible that the positive relation between OCBs and unit effectiveness is spurious. For example, high-performing groups might report that they engage in a great deal of citizenship behavior not because they really do, but because their implicit theories of performance suggest that high-performing groups help each other, are good sports, and exhibit civic virtue. This would be consistent with Staw's (1975) finding that groups who were told that their performance was high rated themselves as more cohesive than groups who were told that their performance was low—even though the feedback was unrelated to the groups' actual performance. Thus, future research designed to more clearly establish the causal direction of relations between these variables is needed.

Other Forms of Extra-Role Behavior

Anticitizenship behaviors. Another interesting direction for future research would be to examine additional forms of extra-role behavior and their impact on unit effectiveness. Fisher and Locke (1992) identified several forms of "anticitizenship behaviors" (ACBs), which might also be expected to influence unit effectiveness. According to Fisher and Locke, ACBs include defiance and resistance to authority (e.g., deliberately ignoring rules, regulations, and/or supervisor's instructions; talking back to the supervisor; purposely interfering with someone else doing his or her job; etc.); revenge/retaliation (e.g., selling company information to competitors; leaking detrimental information to the press; stealing supplies, tools, or company merchandise; etc.); and avoidance from the work itself (e.g., doing as little work as possible; trying to look busy doing nothing; conducting personal business when supposed to be working; etc.). Ball et al. (1994) examined certain antecedents of anticitizenship behavior, but no one has examined the impact of these behaviors on unit effectiveness, even though one would expect many of them to have a negative impact. Thus, future research should investigate this possibility.

Customer-oriented behaviors. In addition to examining the impact of extra-role behaviors that are not necessarily functional for the organization (e.g., ACBs), future research might also examine the impact of extra-role behaviors that are more "customer-oriented" (COBs) as well. Figure 1 identifies four main classes of behaviors that differ based on whether the behavior is in the job description, explicitly rewarded/punished, trained, and so forth, and whether the behavior primarily benefits the organization (or people within the organization) or the organization's customers. As shown in the figure, "in-role" behaviors directed at the "company/organization" are called "work-oriented" behaviors; "in-role" behaviors directed at "customers" are "sales/service-oriented"; "extra-role" behaviors directed at the "company/organization" are "organizational citizenship behaviors"; and "extra-role" behaviors directed at "customers" are "customer-oriented" behav-

	Company-Directed	Customer-Directed
In-Role	Work-Oriented Behaviors (WOB)	Sales/Service Oriented Behaviors (SOB)
Extra-Role	Organizational Citizenship Behaviors (OCB) Anti-Citizenship Behaviors (ACB)	Customer Oriented Behaviors (COB)

FIGURE 1 Employee behavior typology.

iors. All four of these forms of behavior might be expected to influence unit effectiveness. The in-role forms of behavior (i.e., work-directed and sales/service-oriented behaviors) would be expected to influence unit effectiveness for obvious reasons because they relate to the performance of essential job responsibilities; we have already reviewed evidence documenting the impact of OCBs on organizational performance. However, evidence of the impact of customer-oriented behavior is only just beginning to accumulate.

For example, a recent study by George and Bettenhausen (1990) examined the relation between pooled unit-level ratings of customer-oriented prosocial behavior and several objective sales performance in a chain of national retail stores. The customer-oriented behavior measures tapped aspects of customer service and the extent to which the sales associates exhibited helpful behaviors directed toward customers. George and Bettenhausen found that customer-oriented behavior was correlated .33 with unit sales performance, and –.29 with voluntary turnover.

In another study, Narver and Slater (1990) examined the relation between customer orientation and several measures of business performance, among 113 strategic business units in a forest products division of a major corporation. Their measure of customer orientation captured customer commitment, in the process creating customer value, understanding customer needs, and after-sales service. Narver and Slater found that customer orientation was positively related to return on assets ($r = .30$), low cost-based competitive advantage ($r = .27$), and differentiation-based competitive advantage ($r = .44$).

More recently, Kizilos and Cummings (1996) examined the extent to which prosocial organizational behavior mediates the impact of employee involvement on organizational performance in a sample 143 units of large consumer products company. One aspect of each unit's prosocial organizational behavior was called "customer-centered behavior" and reflected anticipating and adapting to customer needs, exceeding customer expectations, and resolving customer problems. They found that customer-centered behavior was positively related ($r = .31$) to a measure of unit sales volume.

Taken together, the empirical evidence from these three studies (George & Bettenhausen, 1990; Kizilos & Cummings, 1996; Narver & Slater, 1990) indicates that customer-oriented behavior may have important effects on unit performance. Although this evidence is far from conclusive, it suggests several priorities for future research. First, because each of these studies defined customer-oriented behavior in different ways, future research needs to focus on identifying the dimensions of COB and more clearly articulate the difference between this type of behavior and "sales/service-oriented" behavior. Second, the impact of COBs on performance should be examined in the context of the effects of in-role behavior and OCB, in order to gain a better understanding of their relative contribution to organizational success. Third, because the evidence reviewed earlier is all correlational in nature, future COB research should attempt to obtain better evidence of the direction of causality between COBs and unit performance, perhaps through experimental or longitudinal research. Finally, future research should attempt to identify moderators of the relation between COB and unit performance.

Other Criterion Variables

A final interesting direction for future research would be to examine the impact of OCB on a broader range of criterion variables. The study by Walz and Niehoff (1996) took an important step in this direction. However, much more research is needed. It might be particularly interesting to examine relations between OCB and employee turnover/retention, customer satisfaction, customer complaints, customer retention, the cost of producing goods/services, return on investment, profitability, innovativeness, adaptability, and so forth. In principle, the synergies created by OCB may have widespread consequences for organizations.

One could argue the same point for other forms of extra-role behavior such as ACBs and COBs. After all, Narver and Slater (1990) have already reported that a form of COB (their "customer-orientation" construct) is positively related to a construct called *human resources management effectiveness* ($r = .44$), and it would not be too surprising if ACBs like "defiance and resistance to authority" or "revenge/retaliation" were found to be negatively related to this construct. Similarly, it might be reasonable to expect that COBs would influence customer satisfaction, customer complaints, customer retention, sales volume, profitability, return on investment, and so on. Thus, although the specific consequences of COBs and ACBs may be somewhat different than the consequences of OCBs, the possibility that other forms of extra-role behavior may have important consequences for organizations is intriguing.

CONCLUSION

The widespread interest in the topic of OCB has been predicated on the assumption that OCBs influence organizational success. Our review of the literature indicates that this assumption has generally been confirmed by empirical data. However, it is important to note that (a) the impact helping behavior on organizational effectiveness appears to be stronger and more consistent than the effects of other forms of citizenship behavior and (b) research on this aspect of citizenship behavior is still in its infancy and the available evidence comes primarily from only four studies. In view of this, additional research is needed to further clarify the impact of OCBs on organizational success and to investigate the other research issues discussed.

REFERENCES

Bagozzi, R. P., Yi, Y., & Phillips, L. W. (1991). Assessing construct validity in organizational research. *Administrative Science Quarterly, 36,* 421–458.

Ball, G. A., Trevino, L. K., & Sims, H. P., Jr. (1994). Just and unjust punishment: Influences on subordinate performance and citizenship. *Academy of Management Journal, 37,* 299–322.

Bateman, T. S., & Organ, D. W. (1983). Job satisfaction and the good soldier: The relationship between affect and employee "citizenship." *Academy of Management Journal, 26,* 587–595.

Berman J. S., & Kenny, D. A. (1976). Correlational bias in observer ratings. *Journal of Personality and Social Psychology, 34,* 263–273.

Borman, W. C., & Motowidlo, S. J. (1993). Expanding the criterion domain to include elements of contextual performance. In N. Schmitt, W. C. Borman, & Associates (Eds.), *Personnel selection in organizations* (pp. 71–98). San Francisco: Jossey-Bass.

Brief, A. P., & Motowidlo, S. J. (1986). Prosocial organizational behaviors. *Academy of Management Review, 10,* 710–725.

Bruner, J. S., & Tagiuri, R. (1954). The perception of people. In G. Lindzey (Ed.), *Handbook of social psychology* (Vol. 2, pp. 634–654). Cambridge, MA: Addison-Wesley.

Farh, J. L., Podsakoff, P. M, & Organ, D. W. (1990). Accounting for organizational citizenship behavior: Leader fairness and task scope versus satisfaction. *Journal of Management, 16,* 705–721.

Fisher, C. D., & Locke, E. A. (1992). The new look in job satisfaction research and theory. In C. J. Cranny, P. C. Smith, & E. F. Stone (Eds.), *Job satisfaction: How people feel about their jobs and how it affects their performance* (pp. 165–194). Lexington, MA: D. C. Heath.

George, J. M. (1990). Personality, affect, and behavior in groups. *Journal of Applied Psychology, 75,* 107–116.

George, J. M., & Bettenhausen, K. (1990). Understanding prosocial behavior, sales performance, and turnover: A group-level analysis in a service context. *Journal of Applied Psychology, 75,* 698–709.

Karambayya, R. (1990). *Contexts for organizational citizenship behavior: Do high performing and satisfying units have better "citizens"* (Working paper). York University, North York, Ontario, Canada.

Kizilos, M. A., & Cummings, T. G. (1996). *Employee involvement, prosocial organizational behavior, and organization performance* (Working paper). University of Alberta, Edmonton, Canada.

MacKenzie, S. B., Podsakoff, P. M., & Ahearne, M. (1996). Unpublished data analysis. Indiana University, Bloomington.

MacKenzie, S. B., Podsakoff, P. M., & Fetter, R. (1991). Organizational citizenship behavior and objective productivity as determinants of managerial evaluations of salespersons' performance. *Organizational Behavior and Human Decision Processes, 50,* 123–150.

MacKenzie, S. B., Podsakoff, P. M., & Fetter, R. (1993). The impact of organizational citizenship behavior on evaluations of salesperson performance. *Journal of Marketing, 57,* 70–80.

Moorman, R. H. (1991). Relationship between organizational justice and organizational citizenship behaviors: Do fairness perceptions influence employee citizenship? *Journal of Applied Psychology, 76,* 845–855.

Munene, J. C. (1995). "Not-on-Seat": An investigation of some correlates of organizational citizenship behavior in Nigeria. *Applied Psychology: An International Review, 44*(2), 111–122.

Narver, J. C., & Slater, S. F. (1990). The effect of a market orientation on business profitability. *Journal of Marketing, 54,* 20–35.

Niehoff, B. P., & Moorman, R. H. (1993). Justice as a mediator of the relationship between methods of monitoring and organizational citizenship behavior. *Academy of Management Journal, 36,* 527–556.

Organ, D. W. (1988). *Organizational citizenship behavior: The good soldier syndrome.* Lexington, MA: Lexington.

Organ, D. W. (1990). The subtle significance of job satisfaction. *Clinical Laboratory Management Review, 4,* 94–98.

Organ, D. W., & Konovsky, M. (1989). Cognitive versus affective determinants of organizational citizenship behavior. *Journal of Applied Psychology, 74,* 157–164.

Organ, D. W., & Ryan, K. (1995). A meta-analytic review of attitudinal and dispositional predictors of organizational citizenship behavior. *Personnel Psychology, 48,* 775–802.

Podsakoff, P. M., Ahearne, M., & MacKenzie, S. B. (in press). Organizational citizenship behavior and the quantity and quality of work group performance. *Journal of Applied Psychology.*

Podsakoff, P. M., & MacKenzie, S. B. (1994). Organizational citizenship behavior and sales unit effectiveness. *Journal of Marketing Research, 31,* 351–363.

Podsakoff, P. M., MacKenzie, S. B., & Bommer, W. (1996a). Transformational leader behaviors and substitutes for leadership as determinants of employee satisfaction, commitment, trust, and organizational citizenship behaviors. *Journal of Management, 22,* 259–298.

Podsakoff, P. M., MacKenzie, S. B., & Bommer, W. H. (1996b). Meta-analysis of the relationships between Kerr and Jermier's substitutes for leadership and employee job attitudes, role perceptions, and performance. *Journal of Applied Psychology, 81,* 380–399.

Podsakoff, P. M., MacKenzie, S. B., & Fetter, R. (1993, Spring). Substitutes for leadership and the management of professionals. *Leadership Quarterly, 4,* 1–44.

Podsakoff, P. M., MacKenzie, S. B., & Hui, C. (1993). Organizational citizenship behaviors as determinants of managerial evaluations of employee performance: A review and suggestions for future research. In G. R. Ferris & K. M. Rowland (Eds.), *Research in personnel and human resources management* (Vol. 11, pp. 1–40). Greenwich, CT: JAI.

Podsakoff, P. M., MacKenzie, S. B., Moorman, R. H., & Fetter, R. (1990). Transformational leader behaviors and their effects on followers' trust in leader, satisfaction, and organizational citizenship behavior. *Leadership Quarterly, 1,* 107–42.

Podsakoff, P. M., Niehoff, B. P., MacKenzie, S. B., & Williams, M. L. (1993). Do substitutes for leadership really substitute for leadership? An empirical examination of Kerr and Jermier's situational leadership model. *Organizational Behavior and Human Decision Processes, 54,* 1–44.

Puffer, S. M. (1987). Prosocial behavior, noncompliant behavior, and work performance among commission salespeople. *Journal of Applied Psychology, 72,* 615–621.

Schnake, M. (1991). Organizational citizenship: A review, proposed model, and research agenda. *Human Relations, 44,* 735–759.

Skarlicki, D. P., & Latham, G. P. (1996). Increasing citizenship behavior within a labor union: A test of organizational justice theory. *Journal of Applied Psychology, 81,* 161–169.

Smith, C. A., Organ, D. W., & Near, J. P. (1983). Organizational citizenship behavior: Its nature and antecedents. *Journal of Applied Psychology, 68,* 655–663.

Staw, B. M., (1975). Attribution of the "causes" of performance: A general alternative interpretation of cross-sectional research on organizations. *Organizational Behavior and Human Decision Processes, 13,* 414–432.

Thompson, J. D. (1967). *Organizations in action.* New York: McGraw-Hill.

Walz, S. M., & Niehoff, B. P. (1996). Organizational citizenship behaviors and their effect on organizational effectiveness in limited-menu restaurants. In J. B. Keys & L. N. Dosier (Eds.), *Academy of Management best papers proceedings* (pp. 307–311). Briarcliff Manor, NY: Academy of Managment.

Williams, L. J., & Anderson, S. E. (1991). Job satisfaction and organizational commitment as predictors of organizational citizenship and in-role behavior. *Journal of Management, 17,* 601–617.

HUMAN PERFORMANCE, *10*(2), 153–170

Organizational Spontaneity in Context

Jennifer M. George and Gareth R. Jones
Department of Management
Texas A&M University

This article suggests that our understanding of extra-role behaviors such as organizational spontaneity may be enhanced by considering the context in which these behaviors occur. The context may provide individuals with either opportunities to engage in forms of organizational spontaneity or constraints against performing these behaviors. Proposed contextual influences at the individual level of analysis include skill level, self-efficacy, role definitions, interpersonal relationships, and help-seeking behavior. Proposed contextual influences at the group level of analysis are group norms, interdependence, and goals. Proposed contextual influences at the organizational level of analysis include organizational structure, culture, company policies, and reward systems. Lastly, proposed contextual influences at the interorganizational level of analysis include the isomorphic forces that result in organizations becoming more similar to each other over time. Implications of this analysis for future theorizing and research are discussed.

Research on organizational spontaneity and related constructs such as organizational citizenship behavior, prosocial organizational behavior, and contextual performance has tended to focus on the relationship between organizational members' personal characteristics, feelings, thoughts, and attitudes, on the one hand, and the extent to which they perform extra-role behaviors on the other. This literature implicitly assumes that people's personal characteristics and reactions in and to the workplace influence the extent to which they will go above and beyond the call of duty. For example, in their model of organizational spontaneity, George and Brief (1992) posited that positive mood at work is a primary antecedent of organizational spontaneity. As another example, organizational citizenship behavior researchers have pinpointed work attitudes and fairness cognitions as key antecedents of these behaviors (e.g., Organ, 1988; Smith, Organ, & Near, 1983).

Requests for reprints should be sent to Jennifer M. George, Department of Management, Texas A&M University, College Station, TX 77843–4221.

Although more research is needed to understand how, when, and why workplace reactions such as job satisfaction or positive mood may culminate in the performance of extra-role behaviors, existing research leads to two tentative conclusions. First, both moods and attitudes do appear to show some relation to these behaviors (e.g., George, 1991; George & Brief, 1992; Organ, 1988; Organ & Ryan, 1995). Second, these relations are not especially strong. For example, in their recent meta-analysis of attitudinal predictors of organizational citizenship behavior, Organ and Ryan (1995) found that job satisfaction was correlated .24 with altruism and .22 with generalized compliance, altruism and generalized compliance being two of the most commonly studied dimensions of organizational citizenship behavior.

Here, we suggest that our understanding of extra-role behaviors such as organizational spontaneity may be enhanced by considering the context in which these behaviors occur. By context, we mean the set of forces stemming from the environment and the person that impact behavior in the work setting. In contrast to much of the existing literature that seeks to identify primary or direct antecedents of these behaviors at the individual level of analysis (such as moods or attitudes), this article explores how the context in which organizational spontaneity occurs serves to encourage or discourage these behaviors. The article unfolds as follows. First, the organizational spontaneity construct is briefly described. Next, we discuss the nature of the contextual forces proposed to affect organizational spontaneity. Proposed contextual forces at four levels of analysis are then described. Finally, implications and directions for future research are discussed.

ORGANIZATIONAL SPONTANEITY

Building from the work of Katz (1964), George and Brief (1992) defined *organizational spontaneity* as voluntarily performed extra-role behaviors that contribute to organizational effectiveness.[1] Five forms of organizational spontaneity are: helping coworkers, protecting the organization, making constructive suggestions, developing oneself, and spreading goodwill. Based on Katz (1964) and George and Brief (1992), these five forms of organizational spontaneity are briefly described following.

Helping coworkers includes all voluntary forms of assistance that organizational members provide each other to facilitate the accomplishment of tasks and attainment of goals. Helping coworkers includes behaviors ranging from helping a coworker with a heavy work load and sharing resources, to calling attention to errors

---

[1]Although the term "spontaneous" is sometimes used to refer to impulsive acts, consistent with George and Brief (1992) and Katz (1964), our use of the term here does not imply that behavior is impulsive. The five forms of organizational spontaneity can be (and are often likely to be) preceded by forethought. They are spontaneous in that they are performed voluntarily or of one's free will.

and omissions and providing instruction in the use of new technology when one is not required to do so. Taking the initiative to help a coworker solve a problem is a spontaneous act that often is not or cannot be assigned in advance.

Protecting the organization includes those voluntary acts organizational members engage in to protect or save life and property ranging from reporting fire hazards, securely locking doors, and reporting suspicious or dangerous activities, to taking the initiative to halt a production process when there is the potential for human injury. This form of organizational spontaneity also includes safeguarding organizational resources.

Making constructive suggestions includes all voluntary acts of creativity and innovation in organizations. Such suggestions can range from the relatively mundane (a more efficient way to handle paper work) to the more monumental (a reorganization of an entire unit to better serve a changing customer base). Rather than just performing their jobs within the realm of the status quo, workers who engage in this form of organizational spontaneity go one step further and actively try to find ways to improve individual, group, or organizational functioning.

Developing oneself includes all the steps that workers take to voluntarily improve their knowledge, skills, and abilities so as to be better able to contribute to their organizations. Seeking out and taking advantage of advanced-training courses, keeping abreast of the latest developments in one's field and area, or even learning a new set of skills so as to expand the range of one's contributions to an organization are included in this form of spontaneity.

Lastly, spreading goodwill is the means by which organizational members voluntarily contribute to organizational effectiveness through efforts to represent their organizations to wider communities in a beneficial light. Whether it be describing one's organization as supportive and caring or describing an organization's goods and services as being high quality and responsive to customers' needs, instances of spreading goodwill contribute to organizational effectiveness by ensuring that organizations obtain needed resources from various stakeholder groups.

As mentioned earlier, organizational spontaneity is related to the constructs of prosocial organizational behavior (Brief & Motowidlo, 1986), organizational citizenship behavior (Organ, 1988), and contextual performance (Borman & Motowidlo, 1993; Motowidlo & Van Scotter, 1994). Although there is obvious overlap between these four constructs, there are important differences (George & Brief, 1992). For example, prosocial organizational behavior differs from organizational spontaneity in that it includes behaviors that are dysfunctional for an organization (but help another individual), role-prescribed behaviors, and passive behaviors such as remaining with an organization. As another example, organizational citizenship behaviors differ from organizational spontaneity in that some organizational citizenship behaviors are role-prescribed such as attendance and punctuality, whereas others are passive such as avoiding complaining. Citizenship also differs from spontaneity in that citizenship behaviors cannot be recognized by an organization's reward system. In this article we concentrate on the effects of context on organizational spontaneity, but the substantial overlap between these four constructs implies that similar conjectures might be made with regards to prosocial organizational behavior, organizational citizenship behavior, and contextual performance.

CONTEXT

Although there have been repeated calls for more attention to context in the organizational behavior literature (e.g., Cappelli & Sherer, 1991; Cummings, 1981; Mowday & Sutton, 1993; O'Reilly, 1991; Wilpert, 1995), context continues to be a relatively underexplored explanatory factor, with the literature on organizational spontaneity being no exception. Cappelli and Sherer (1991, p. 56) defined context as "the surroundings associated with phenomena that help to illuminate that phenomena, typically factors associated with units of analysis above those expressly under investigation."

Organizational spontaneity, while referring to individual behavior, occurs in the context of group and organizational memberships. Individuals who perform or fail to perform spontaneous behaviors are not doing so in a vacuum and it is likely that the group and organizational context in which these behaviors are performed serves to encourage or discourage them.

Whereas context is usually viewed as environmental forces or organizational characteristics at a higher level of analysis that affect a focal behavior in question (e.g., Cappelli & Sherer, 1991), in this article we take a broad view of context such that it also includes forces at the individual level of analysis. These contextual forces at the individual level of analysis are distinguished from individual antecedents of spontaneity (such as positive mood) because they are not so much direct causes of spontaneity but rather serve to encourage or discourage spontaneity even when facilitating factors such as positive mood are present. Thus, as proposed in this article, the context of organizational spontaneity incorporates forces at four different levels of analysis: individual, group, organizational, and interorganizational (Figure 1).

An appropriate way to explore the effects of context with respect to organizational spontaneity is to study the extent to which context provides individuals with opportunities to be spontaneous or introduces constraints against being spontaneous (Blau, 1987; Huber, 1990; Mowday & Sutton, 1993). At the individual level of analysis, characteristics of individuals and their relationships with others may provide them with opportunities to be spontaneous or may constrain their efforts to be spontaneous. Similarly, work group, organizational, and interorganizational forces may constrain organizational spontaneity or provide opportunities for its occurrence. Although a multitude of contextual factors at these four levels of

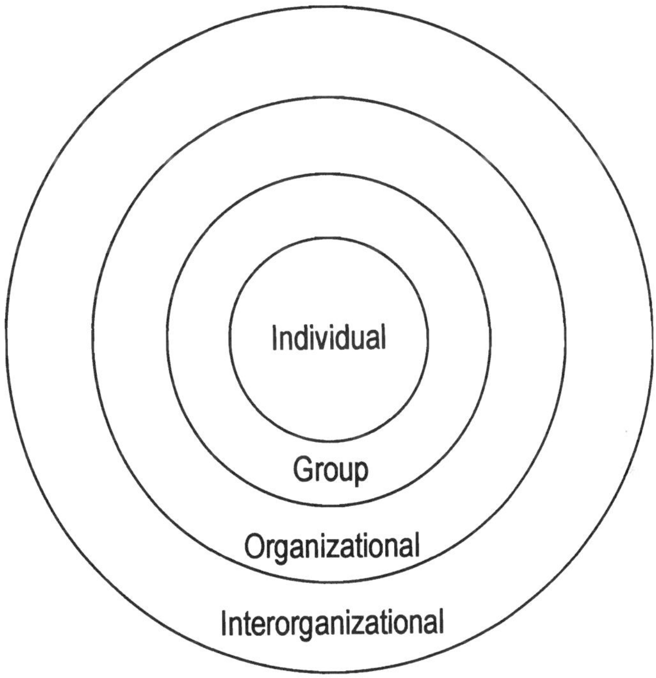

FIGURE 1 Four levels of context.

analysis have the potential to facilitate or discourage organizational spontaneity, based on reviews of relevant literatures, we have chosen a few contextual factors at each level of analysis that we believe may be especially important. Following, we describe these factors and their potential for providing opportunities or constraints for spontaneity. It is important to keep in mind that there are likely other important contextual forces on organizational spontaneity that we have neglected to consider. Hopefully, the following analysis will prompt other researchers to both consider the role of context for behaviors like organizational spontaneity and to identify other potentially important contextual forces.

Individual Context of Organizational Spontaneity

Although individual characteristics such as mood states, attitudes, and dispositions have been theorized to be determinants of organizational spontaneity and related constructs such as organizational citizenship (e.g., George, 1991; George & Brief, 1992; Organ, 1988; Organ & Ryan, 1995), regardless of a person's standing on these characteristics, it is likely that certain other characteristics at the individual level of analysis provide either opportunities or constraints for organizational spontaneity, and thus serve as contextual influences at the individual level. Five such contextual influences are considered here: skill level, self-efficacy, role definition, interpersonal relationships, and help-seeking behavior.

Skill level. Suppose that an individual experiences positive moods at work; has positive attitudes toward the organization, the job, coworkers, and supervisors; and perceives that he or she is being treated fairly. The literature suggests that such a person may be more likely to be helpful to coworkers than a person with less positive workplace reactions (e.g., George & Brief, 1992; Organ & Ryan, 1995). Suppose, however, that this person has the least tenure in a work group and the lowest level of skill, knowledge, and experience of all other group members. Even though this person has the moods, attitudes, and cognitions that should encourage helpfulness, this person, while exuding a pleasant demeanor, may not be especially helpful to coworkers in providing them assistance with work tasks because a low skill level constrains his or her ability to be helpful. In contrast, a worker who is especially knowledgeable may have many opportunities to be helpful. People who have expertise in computer software and hardware, for example, often have multiple opportunities to help others even though their own jobs per se are not concerned with computer technology.

Skill level is also likely to constrain or encourage other forms of organizational spontaneity in addition to helping coworkers. For example, workers with low skill levels may have different kinds of opportunities for self-development than workers with high skills levels. As another example, the extent to which an organizational member spreads goodwill about the organization might be constrained by the member's actual knowledge of organizational practices and products.

Self-efficacy. Wood and Bandura (1989a, p. 408) defined *self-efficacy* as "beliefs in one's capabilities to mobilize the motivation, cognitive resources, and courses of action needed to meet given situational demands." Gist and Mitchell (1992) suggested that three major aspects of self-efficacy are highlighted in this definition and the wider body of literature on self-efficacy (e.g., Bandura, 1982, 1988; Bandura & Wood, 1989; Wood & Bandura, 1989b). First, self-efficacy is a global judgment of one's ability to perform a specific task or behavior. Second, self-efficacy can change over time. And third, self-efficacy can be an activating force for behavior.

Although self-efficacy has been linked to performance in a wide variety of organizational contexts (e.g., Barling & Beattie, 1983; Taylor, Locke, Lee, & Gist, 1984), it is likely that self-efficacy also influences the performance of extra-role behaviors such as organizational spontaneity. Because self-efficacy is task-specific, individuals may have varying levels of self-efficacy for each of the five forms of organizational spontaneity. And it is likely that high self-efficacy will create more opportunities for spontaneity and low self efficacy will constrain spontaneity. If individuals feel unable to offer useful help to a coworker, no matter how positive their moods or attitudes are, such help is not likely to be forthcoming. Similarly, if individuals feel that they will not be able to successfully complete an advanced training course, then they are unlikely to take it of their own free will. Individuals with high self-efficacy may make more constructive suggestions because they believe they can provide creative solutions to problems as well as input on new opportunities. In fact, self-efficacy is likely to constrain or encourage each of the five forms of organizational spontaneity. For example, Noe and Wilk (1993) found self-efficacy to be positively related to self-reported self-development activities. Again, it should be stressed that any given individual may have varying levels of self-efficacy for each of the forms of organizational spontaneity. For example, a person could have high self-efficacy for self-development activities yet low self-efficacy for protecting the organization.

Role definition. The boundary between in-role and extra-role behaviors is a fuzzy one and people may differ in terms of how they define their roles (Graen, 1976; Morrison, 1994; Rousseau, 1989). At one extreme, an individual may define a role so narrowly that certain activities are avoided because they are not formally or explicitly required even though they may be necessary for effective job performance. At another extreme, an individual may define a role so broadly that it includes all of the five forms of organizational spontaneity. For such an individual, these behaviors are not perceived to be voluntary but mandatory. In a sample of clerical employees, Morrison (1994) found that when workers defined their roles more broadly, they were more likely to engage in organizational citizenship behaviors. Building from her findings, it is likely that when individuals define their own roles broadly, they will be more likely to find opportunities to perform forms of organizational spontaneity. In contrast, narrow role definitions are likely to constrain spontaneity.

Although role definition is viewed here as a contextual factor at the individual level of analysis, contextual factors at higher levels of analysis are likely to influence how an individual perceives his or her own role. For example, at the work group level, social influence from coworkers is likely to impact an individual's role definition. At the organizational level, norms and values that are part of a strong organizational culture may impact how individuals define their own roles.

Interpersonal relationships. The helping coworkers form of organizational spontaneity has been the focus of, perhaps, the most research attention. The nature of the interpersonal relationship between the help giver and help provider is likely to influence the extent of helping coworkers in the workplace. Clearly, people are less likely to help people whom they dislike or disrespect and are more likely to help people with whom they have a positive interpersonal relationship. However, the nature of interpersonal relationships may have a more subtle influence on helping coworkers.

Research on interpersonal relationships has identified two types of relationships that have different implications for helping behavior, communal relationships and exchange relationships (Clark & Mills, 1979; Mills & Clark, 1982). In communal relationships, people feel more responsible for each other's well-being, desire to help each other, and feel obligated to help each other out when the need arises (Clark, Ouellette, Powell, & Milberg, 1987). Exchange relationships are characterized by a more quid pro quo orientation to helping. Help is provided to recompense help received in the past or help to be provided in the future. Clark et al. (1987) theorized and found that when an individual perceived that he or she had a communal relationship with another person, they were more likely to help them. In work settings, it is likely that individuals may develop communal relationships with some of their coworkers and exchange relationships with others. Based on the theorizing of Clark, Mills, and colleagues (e.g., Clark & Mills, 1979; Clark et al., 1987; Mills & Clark, 1982), one would expect communal relationships with coworkers to provide increased opportunities for helping and exchange relationship with coworkers to act as constraints on helping.

Help-seeking behavior. Help-seeking behavior on the part of potential recipients of helping may be an additional factor that influences the occurrence of helping coworkers. Research has found that helping in organizations is frequently initiated by a request for help on the part of potential recipients (Burke, Weir, & Duncan, 1976; Kaplan & Cowen, 1981). More recently, Anderson and Williams (1996) found, in a sample of hospital workers, that help seeking by coworkers was positively associated with actual helping behavior. Help-seeking clearly provides organizational members with an opportunity to engage in extra-role behaviors like helping. When organizational members refrain from seeking help, they may constrain helping simply because others might not be aware of their needs. People may refrain from seeking help for a number of reasons including not wanting to appear deficient or inadequate, not wanting to admit to oneself that help is needed, wanting to maintain one's independence and not have it threatened, and not having to feel indebted to another person or feel the need to reciprocate in the future (e.g., Brehm, 1966; Greenberg, 1980; Nadler, 1991; Walster, Walster, & Berscheid, 1978).

It is likely that these and other contextual characteristics at the individual level of analysis serve to provide opportunities for or constraints against organizational spontaneity.

The Group Context of Organizational Spontaneity

Although organizational spontaneity as a construct is concerned with individual acts of helping coworkers, protecting the organization, making constructive suggestions, developing oneself, and spreading goodwill, these individual acts occur in the context of membership in primary work groups. Work group characteristics may serve to provide opportunities for spontaneity or constraints against it. In particular, group norms, interdependence, and goals may be important aspects of the group context of organizational spontaneity.

Group norms. Hackman (1992, p. 235) defined *norms* as "structural characteristics of groups that summarize and simplify group influence processes." Norms specify behaviors that are deemed to be important in a group and are the informal rules for behavior that most group members follow. We propose that work groups may be likely to develop norms surrounding the five forms of organizational spontaneity. In some groups, it may be an agreed upon norm that group members always help each other out. In other groups, members may feel under no implicit obligation to be helpful. Similarly, some groups may have norms supportive of creativity and innovation, whereas others may have norms supportive of a "don't rock the boat; if it ain't broke, don't fix it" mentality. Likewise group norms may be differentially supportive of self-development activities, protection of the organization, and spreading goodwill. For example, some groups may emphasize the need to conserve organizational resources (a way of protecting the organization), whereas other groups may view organizational resources as free goods that group members should take advantage of to the fullest.

Group norms that are supportive of organizational spontaneity will obviously encourage group members to engage in these kinds of behaviors while norms that do not support or discourage organizational spontaneity will obviously constrain such behaviors. At this point, a critic might counter that if groups do develop norms that dictate that groups members are expected to display certain forms of organizational spontaneity, then the behavior is no longer spontaneous or performed of one's free will. There is a certain merit to such an argument; yet to deny the role of norms as an important contextual influence on spontaneity on these grounds may be misguided. That is, it is possible that group members perceive that certain behaviors actually are voluntarily performed (i.e., are extra-role and do not need to be performed vis-à-vis the larger organization), yet, as a group, members perceive these behaviors to be important and seek to encourage their performance through the development of group norms.

Take the hypothetical case of two different academic departments in a university. Although professors in each department are expected to perform teaching, research, and service activities, and professors in both departments generally tend to excel on these three role-prescribed activities, professors in the first department also perform many of the forms of organizational spontaneity (e.g., they are very helpful to each other; they strive to make improvements not only in the functioning of the department but also their college and the university as a whole; they continually develop and expand their knowledge and skills; they are protective of their department and university; and they are good-will ambassadors for their university in their interactions with students, alumni, donors, and fellow academicians). Members of the second department do not tend to perform these activities yet are nonetheless excellent teachers, researchers, and service contributors. Members of the first department may not feel so much that they must perform these behaviors but rather that they want to as it is the group itself that has deemed these behaviors to be important enough to warrant the development of group norms.

Consistent with the idea that group norms may be supportive of spontaneity is evidence that groups may have climates for organizational spontaneity or climates for the various forms of spontaneity (Schneider, 1975; Schneider & Reichers, 1983). For example, it has been suggested that there can be a climate for innovation (Scott & Bruce, 1994), and work units can differ according to how supportive they are of self-development activities (Noe & Wilk, 1993).

Interdependence. The nature of the work activities of a group determines the level of interdependence between group members. Thompson's (1967) tripartite classification of task interdependence provides a useful starting place for examining task interdependence in groups. This classification scheme describes three major types of task interdependence: pooled, sequential, and reciprocal. With pooled interdependence, group members essentially work independently of each other and combine their end products. With sequential interdependence, work activities must be performed in a predetermined order such as on an assembly line. With reciprocal interdependence, each group members' activities are fully dependent on the activities of other group members (Thompson, 1967).

The level of interdependence among group members is likely to be an important contextual influence for at least two of the five forms of organizational spontaneity. High levels of interdependence among group members (e.g., reciprocal interdependence) is likely to provide increased opportunities for both helping coworkers and making constructive suggestions. In contrast, when interdependence is low, helping may be constrained as group members work independently of each other. Similarly, making constructive suggestions may be constrained as group members' are narrowly focused on their own work activities.

Consistent with this reasoning, Pearce and Gregersen (1991) found that interdependence resulted in people feeling more responsibility to perform extra-role behaviors and felt responsibility, in turn, was positively associated with actual performance of extra-role behaviors. Also consistent with this reasoning is a model of helping behavior proposed and tested by Anderson and Williams (1996). In their model, task interdependence was found to positively influence help-seeking behavior that in turn promoted helping.

Goals. Goals, as a contextual influence on organizational spontaneity, can operate both at the individual and the group levels of analysis. At the individual level of analysis, specific, difficult goals assigned to individuals may serve to constrain organizational spontaneity. Specific, difficult goals are by definition hard to achieve and revolve around role-prescribed behaviors. The goals serve to both channel behavior toward the accomplishment of prescribed tasks and focus attention and increased effort on these tasks. Organizational spontaneity may be perceived to, and may actually, detract from individual goal attainment. Time spent helping a coworker, making a constructive suggestion, or pursuing self-development, for example, is time not spent on striving to obtain a goal. Consistent with this reasoning are studies that explore the effects that goals have both on behavior specified in the goal and on behaviors not specified by the goal. Bavelas and Lee (1978), for example, found that quantity goals resulted in increased performance in terms of quantity but decreased performance in terms of quality. Staw and Boettger (1990) found that people assigned specific goals were less likely to modify or revise tasks and behaviors even when the behaviors were inappropriate. Shalley (1991) found that when performance goals were assigned (and creativity goals were not assigned), creativity suffered. As a final example, Wright, George, Farnsworth, and McMahan (1993) found that when people were committed to specific, difficult goals, they were less likely to perform extra-role behaviors.

At the group level of analysis, group goals may serve to encourage certain forms of organizational spontaneity and constrain others. Difficult group goals, for example, may provide opportunities for helping coworkers and making constructive suggestions as these activities may be seen as facilitating group goal accomplishment. Other forms of spontaneity such as protecting the organization and spreading goodwill may be either unaffected by group goals or be constrained by group goals to the extent that these activities are seen as interfering with group goal accomplishment. Using organizational resources in an inefficient manner may help a group achieves its goals, for example, and spreading goodwill may detract from time available to work toward group goal attainment.

These are by no means the only potential contextual influences on organizational spontaneity at the group level of analysis. However, they are suggestive of the range of group characteristics and processes that may serve to constrain or encourage organizational spontaneity. Groups have important effects on their members' performance of role-prescribed behaviors (Hackman, 1992) and it is likely that they also have effects on the extra-role behaviors that group members perform.

Organizational Context of Organizational Spontaneity

Characteristics of whole organizations may also serve to provide opportunities for or constraints against organizational spontaneity, in particular, organizational structure, culture, company policies, and reward systems.

Organizational structure. At a basic level, organizational structures can be distinguished in terms of how mechanistic or organic they are (Burns & Stalker, 1961; Lawrence & Lorsch, 1967; Morand, 1995). Four basic characteristics underlying mechanistic and organic structures are: role specification, distribution of power, coordination of activity, and the nature of commitment (Burns & Stalker, 1961; Lawrence & Lorsch, 1967). Mechanistic structures are characterized by highly specified roles, centralization of power, coordination via the organizational hierarchy, and commitment to the job and function (Burns & Stalker, 1961; Lawrence & Lorsch, 1967). Organic structures, on the other hand, are characterized by loosely specified and changing roles, decentralization of power, coordination by mutual adjustment, and commitment to the organization rather than the job or function (Burns & Stalker, 1961; Lawrence & Lorsch, 1967).

The rigid nature of mechanistic structures and the local orientation (i.e., commitment to job or function) they promote is likely to constrain organizational spontaneity. The highly programmed nature of activities in mechanistic structures along with the centralization of power may cause organizational members to actually be afraid to step out of their assigned roles or perform activities that have not been assigned. By definition, mechanistic structures tend to stifle personal initiative in the interests of control and efficiency.[2]

Organic structures, on the other hand, may provide many opportunities for organizational spontaneity due to their fluid nature and emphasis on adjustment, accommodation, and integration. Loosely specified roles encourage members to take the initiative to respond to changing conditions and do what's best for the organization as a whole. Rather than having an orientation away from organizational spontaneity as is true in a mechanistic structure, organic structures almost create a shared expectation that organizational spontaneity will occur. Consistent with this reasoning, Schneider (1996, p. 557) suggested that behaviors like the five forms of organizational spontaneity are "implicitly demanded more and thus displayed more in organic than in mechanistic systems." Similarly, Morand (1995) suggested that mechanistic structures are characterized by formality and organic structures are characterized by informality. Informality, in turn, leads to more spontaneous behavior (Morand, 1995).

---

[2]Although mechanistic structures have the potential to constrain organizational spontaneity, they also have their advantages such as efficiency, control, and predictability.

Culture. Organizational culture includes the beliefs, norms, and values that are relatively shared in an organization. Culture helps organizational members make sense of organizational life and serves as a guide to action (Trice & Beyer, 1993). It is likely that at least some of the beliefs, norms, and values that make up organizational culture serve to provide opportunities for or constraints against organizational spontaneity. For example, some organizations may value innovation whereas others may value stability and predictability; making constructive suggestions will be encouraged in the former and constrained in the latter. Some organizations may endorse social responsibility values that encourage the spreading of goodwill while others may be more inwardly focused. Some organizations may have a more collective orientation in which helping others and doing what's best for the organization as a whole is emphasized whereas others may be more individualistic or competitive and helping others is constrained to the extent it interferes with individual achievement.

Company policies. At a more mundane level, company policies may constrain or encourage some forms of organizational spontaneity. The clearest example of this would be policies that provide organizational members with reimbursements for expenses associated with self-development activities and time off for such activities. In many organizations with such policies, self-development is a voluntary activity yet it is promoted by providing people with the opportunity to take part in it (by covering part or all of the financial and time burden).

Reward systems. Although a reward system that bases pay on individual performance may be beneficial in terms of ensuring high performance of role-prescribed behaviors (Lawler, 1981), it may inadvertently constrain organizational spontaneity. This is so because performing spontaneous behaviors will rarely contribute to individual performance and may often detract from it such as when time is spent helping coworkers at the expense of completing one's own assignments.

A reward system based on group performance may serve to encourage forms of spontaneity beneficial to work groups (such as helping coworkers, making constructive suggestions, and developing oneself) but may also serve as a constraint on forms of spontaneity beneficial to the organization as a whole (such as spreading goodwill and protecting the organization). Finally, reward systems based on organizational performance may provide opportunities for multiple forms of organizational spontaneity but at the potential expense of lower individual performance and/or increased social loafing (George, 1992; Jones, 1984; Lawler, 1981).

Reward systems are seen as providing opportunities or constraints for spontaneity not because spontaneous behaviors are directly rewarded by the system but rather because the reward system focuses attention toward certain kinds of behaviors and away from others. Individual reward systems focus attention on behaviors that contribute to individual performance and not on those that may contribute to organizational performance. Consistent with this reasoning, Wright et al. (1993) found the lowest level of extra-role behavior to take place when individuals were assigned difficult goals and were rewarded on the basis of individual goal attainment. Also consistent with this reasoning is research that examines the aggregate effects of changes in reward systems. For example, Hatcher and Ross (1991) found that grievances declined and quality levels improved when an organization switched from an individual piece-rate pay plan to an organization-wide gainsharing plan. As another example, Petty, Singleton, and Connell (1992) found that a division of an electric utility that implemented a division-wide incentive plan outperformed a control division on 11 out of 12 performance indicators.

This discussion of the organizational context of organizational spontaneity hopefully suggests some of the ways in which spontaneous behaviors may be encouraged or constrained by organizational characteristics. There are many other potential organizational forces that may serve to encourage or constrain organizational spontaneity. For example, Baron (1994) reviewed an extensive body of literature that suggests aspects of the physical environment of organizations (such as temperature, noise, lighting, air quality, and crowding) have the potential to have wide ranging effects on work behaviors and interpersonal relationships.

Interorganizational Context of Organizational Spontaneity

The interorganizational context can also serve to encourage or constrain organizational spontaneity. As discussed previously, organizational spontaneity does not occur in a vacuum. Rather, these behaviors are performed or fail to be performed within the framework of assumptions and beliefs that govern behavior in a social context. Increasingly, researchers are looking outside the boundaries of an organization, to the interorganizational context, to understand behavior within an organization. Put simply, behavior occurring inside one organization is affected by behavior occurring in other organizations.

In particular, researchers have argued that, over time, organizations become more similar to each other, or isomorphic, because of the operation of coercive, mimetic, and normative forces (Dimaggio & Powell, 1983). When coercive isomorphism takes place, organizations become more similar because they are pressured into adopting certain norms (e.g., people should engage in self-development and be innovative) by other organizations and society as a whole. For example, as part of its commitment to total quality management, Xerox Corporation puts tremendous pressure on its suppliers to do everything they can to increase the quality of their inputs and expects its suppliers to encourage their members to be supportive and helpful toward Xerox's employees.

When mimetic isomorphism takes place, organizations become more similar because they copy each other and imitate what appear to be successful business practices (such as the use of cross-functional teams to improve responsiveness to customers). For example, managers in an engineering consulting firm may encourage their subordinates to seek advanced graduate degrees and certificates. Perceiving that a highly educated workforce is a source of competitive advantage for this firm, managers of competing firms may imitate this practice and encourage their own subordinates to engage in relevant self-development activities.

Lastly, when normative isomorphism takes place, behavior occurring in different organizations becomes more similar over time because organizations and their members indirectly or unconsciously come to adopt the values and norms (such as being helpful to coworkers) of other organizations in their environment.

At a basic level, adaptive extra-role behaviors may percolate through a population of organizations in an environment for at least two reasons. First, many, if not most, organizational members are involved in interorganizational relationships. And second, voluntary and involuntary turnover and hiring practices ensure that a transfer of employees takes place across organizations in an environment. Thus, the interorganizational context serves as a conduit that can spread extra-role behaviors and determine the forms and levels of organizational spontaneity encouraged in any particular organization.

Multiple Roles of Context

Context has the potential to play multiple kinds of roles vis-à-vis organizational spontaneity. Under certain conditions, context may have direct effects such as when an individual incentive plan discourages organizational spontaneity. Alternatively, context may have indirect effects through its impact on workplace reactions such as attitudes and moods. Yet another way that context may play out is in terms of interacting with other antecedents of organizational spontaneity such as moods or attitudes.

Moreover, the same contextual factor may play these different roles simultaneously. For example, a mechanistic organization structure may directly constrain organizational spontaneity and an organic structure may encourage it. A mechanistic structure might also dampen positive moods at work and depress work attitudes, which, in turn, may also lead to low levels of organizational spontaneity, with the converse being true for an organic structure. Finally, relationships between individual reactions such as positive moods and spontaneity may be stronger in organic structures and weaker in mechanistic structures. Obviously, these are conjectures in need of further theorizing and research. But, hopefully they do illustrate that context has the potential to play multiple roles vis-à-vis organizational spontaneity.

IMPLICATIONS

Many if not most of the ideas presented in this article are tentative, given the lack of research on the context of organizational spontaneity and related forms of behavior such as organizational citizenship behavior and contextual performance. Theory-driven empirical research is clearly needed to uncover how contextual factors at the individual, group, organizational, and interorganizational levels of analysis may or may not serve to encourage or constrain the five forms of organizational spontaneity described earlier.

If context is found to have some of the effects posited here, it may help to explain why relationships between hypothesized antecedents of extra-role behaviors and the behaviors themselves have not been especially strong (Organ & Ryan, 1995). For example, contextual effects at the organizational level of analysis may serve to restrict the range of levels of organizational spontaneity observed in any single organization and thus attenuate correlations between organizational spontaneity and hypothesized antecedents at the individual level of analysis.

All in all, we hope that we have at least sparked some interest in exploring the context of organizational spontaneity and other extra-role behaviors. Organizational spontaneity, by definition, occurs in organizations and the nature of those organizations, the groups nested in them, and the people nested in the groups may serve to constrain or encourage organizational members to go above and beyond the call of duty.

REFERENCES

Anderson, S. E., & Williams, L. J. (1996). Interpersonal, job, and individual factors related to helping processes at work. *Journal of Applied Psychology, 81,* 282–296.

Bandura, A. (1982). Self-efficacy mechanism in human agency. *American Psychologist, 37,* 122–147.

Bandura, A. (1988). Self-regulation of motivation and action through goal systems. In V. Hamilton, G. H. Bower, & N. H. Frigda (Eds.), *Cognitive perspectives on emotion and motivation* (pp. 37–61). Dordrecht, The Netherlands: Kluwer.

Bandura, A., & Wood, R. E. (1989). Effect of perceived controllability and performance standards on self-regulation of complex decision making. *Journal of Personality and Social Psychology, 56,* 805–814.

Barling, J., & Beattie, R. (1983). Self-efficacy beliefs and sales performance. *Journal of Organizational Behavior Management, 5,* 41–51.

Baron, R. A. (1994). The physical environment of work settings: Effects on task performance, interpersonal relations, and job satisfaction. In B. M. Staw & L. L. Cummings (Eds.), *Research in organizational behavior* (Vol. 16, pp. 1–46). Greenwich, CT: JAI.

Bavelas, J., & Lee, E. (1978). Effects of goal level on performance: A trade-off of quantity and quality. *Canadian Journal of Psychology, 32,* 219–239.

Blau, P. (1987). Contrasting theoretical perspectives. In J. Alexander, B. Giesen, R. Muench, & N. Smelser (Eds.), *The micro–macro link* (pp. 71–85). Berkeley, CA: University of California Press.

Borman, W. C., & Motowidlo, S. J. (1993). Expanding the criterion domain to include elements of contextual performance. In N. Schmitt & W. C. Borman (Eds.), *Personnel selection in organizations* (71–98). San Francisco: Jossey-Bass.

Brehm, J. W. (1966). *A theory of psychological reactance.* New York: Academic.

Brief, A. P., & Motowidlo, S. J. (1986). Prosocial organizational behaviors. *Academy of Management Review, 11,* 710–725.

Burke, R. J., Weir, T., & Duncan, G. (1976). Informal helping relationships in work organizations. *Academy of Management Journal, 19,* 370–377.

Burns, T., & Stalker, G. M. (1961). *The management of innovation.* London: Tavistock.

Cappelli, P., & Sherer, P. D. (1991). The missing role of context in OB: The need for a meso-level approach. In B. M. Staw & L. L. Cummings (Eds.), *Research in organizational behavior* (Vol. 13, pp. 55–110). Greenwich, CT: JAI.

Clark, M. S., & Mills, J. (1979). Interpersonal attraction in exchange and communal relationships. *Journal of Personality and Social Psychology, 37,* 12–24.

Clark, M. S., Ouellette, R., Powell, M. C., & Milberg, S. (1987). Recipient's mood, relationship type, and helping. *Journal of Personality and Social Psychology, 53,* 94–103.

Cummings, L. L. (1981). Organizational behavior. *Annual Review of Psychology, 33,* 541–579.

Dimaggio, P., & Powell, W. (1983). The iron cage revisited: Institutional isomorphism and collective rationality in organizational fields. *American Sociological Review, 48,* 147–160.

George, J. M. (1991). State or trait: Effects of positive mood on prosocial behaviors at work. *Journal of Applied Psychology, 76,* 299–307.

George, J. M. (1992). Extrinsic and intrinsic origins of perceived social loafing in organizations. *Academy of Management Journal, 35,* 191–202.

George, J. M., & Brief, A. P. (1992). Feeling good-doing good: A conceptual analysis of the mood at work-organizational spontaneity relationship. *Psychological Bulletin, 112,* 310–329.

Gist, M. E., & Mitchell, T. R. (1992). Self-efficacy: A theoretical analysis of its determinants and malleability. *Academy of Management Review, 17,* 183–211.

Graen, G. (1976). Role making processes within complex organizations. In M. D. Dunnette (Ed.), *Handbook of industrial and organizational psychology* (pp. 1201–1245). Chicago: Rand McNally.

Greenberg, M. S. (1980). A theory of indebtedness. In K. J. Gergen, M. S. Greenberg, & R. H. Willis (Eds.), *Social exchange: Advances in theory and research* (pp. 190–210). New York: Plenum.

Hackman, J. R. (1992). Group influences on individuals in organizations. In M. D. Dunnette & L. M. Hough (Eds.), *Handbook of industrial and organizational psychology* (2nd ed., Vol. 3, pp. 199–267). Palo Alto, CA: Consulting Psychologists Press.

Hatcher, L., & Ross, T. L. (1991). From individual incentives to an organization-wide gainsharing plan: Effects on teamwork and product quality. *Journal of Organizational Behavior, 12,* 169–183.

Huber, J. (1990). Macro–micro links in gender stratification. *American Sociological Review, 55,* 1–10.

Jones, G. R. (1984). Task visibility, free riding, and shirking: Explaining the effect of structure and technology on employee behavior. *Academy of Management Review, 9,* 684–695.

Kaplan, E. M., & Cowen, E. L. (1981). Interpersonal helping behavior of industrial foremen. *Journal of Applied Psychology, 66,* 633–638.

Katz, D. (1964). The motivational basis of organizational behavior. *Behavioral Science, 9,* 131–146.

Lawler, E. E. (1981). *Pay and organization development.* Reading, MA: Addison-Wesley.

Lawrence, P. R., & Lorsch, J. W. (1967). *Organization and environment.* Boston: Graduate School of Business Administration, Harvard University.

Mills, J., & Clark, M. S. (1982). Exchange and communal relationships. In L. Wheeler (Ed.), *Review of personality and social psychology* (pp. 121–144). Beverly Hills: Sage.

Morand, D. A. (1995). The role of behavioral formality and informality in the enactment of bureaucratic versus organic organizations. *Academy of Management Review, 20,* 831–872.

Morrison, E. W. (1994). Role definitions and organizational citizenship behavior: The importance of the employee's perspective. *Academy of Management Journal, 37,* 1543–1567.

Motowidlo, S. J., & Van Scotter, J. R. (1994). Evidence that task performance should be distinguished from contextual performance. *Journal of Applied Psychology, 79,* 475–480.

Mowday, R. T., & Sutton, R. I. (1993). Organizational behavior: Linking individuals and groups to organizational contexts. *Annual Review of Psychology, 44,* 195–229.

Nadler, A. (1991). Help-seeking behavior: Psychological costs and instrumental benefits. In M. S. Clark (Ed.), *Prosocial behavior: Review of personality and social psychology* (pp. 290–311). New York: Academic.

Noe, R. A., & Wilk, S. L. (1993). Investigation of the factors that influence employees' participation in development activities. *Journal of Applied Psychology, 78,* 291–302.

O'Reilly, C. A. (1991). Organizational behavior: Where we've been, where we're going. *Annual Review of Psychology, 42,* 427–458.

Organ, D. W. (1988). *Organizational citizenship behavior: The good soldier syndrome.* Lexington, MA: Lexington.

Organ, D. W., & Ryan, K. (1995). A meta-analytic review of attitudinal and dispositional predictors of organizational citizenship behavior. *Personnel Psychology, 48,* 775–802.

Pearce, J. L., & Gregersen, H. B. (1991). Task interdependence and extrarole behavior: A test of the mediating effects of felt responsibility. *Journal of Applied Psychology, 76,* 838–844.

Petty, M. M., Singleton, B., & Connell, D. W. (1992). An experimental evaluation of an organizational incentive plan in the electric utility industry. *Journal of Applied Psychology, 77,* 427–436.

Rousseau, D. M. (1989). Psychological and implied contracts in organizations. *Employee Responsibilities and Rights Journal, 2,* 121–139.

Schneider, B. (1975). Organizational climates: An essay. *Personnel Psychology, 28,* 447–479.

Schneider, B. (1996). When individual differences aren't. In K. R. Murphy (Ed.), *Individual differences and behavior in organizations* (pp. 548–571). San Francisco: Jossey-Bass.

Schneider, B., & Reichers, A. E. (1983). On the etiology of climates. *Personnel Psychology, 36,* 19–39.

Scott, S. G., & Bruce, R. A. (1994). Determinants of innovative behavior: A path model of individual innovation in the workplace. *Academy of Management Journal, 37,* 580–607.

Shalley, C. E. (1991). Effects of productivity goals, creativity goals, and personal discretion on individual creativity. *Journal of Applied Psychology, 76,* 179–185.

Smith, C. A., Organ, D. W., & Near, J. P. (1983). Organizational citizenship behavior: Its nature and antecedents. *Journal of Applied Psychology, 68,* 653–663.

Staw, B. M., & Boettger, R. D. (1990). Task revision: A neglected form of work performance. *Academy of Management Journal, 33,* 534–559.

Taylor, M. S., Locke, E. A., Lee, C., & Gist, M. E. (1984). Type A behavior and faculty research productivity: What are the mechanisms? *Organizational Behavior and Human Decision Processes, 34,* 402–418.

Thompson, J. D. (1967). *Organizations in action.* New York: McGraw-Hill.

Trice, H. M., & Beyer, J. M. (1993). *The cultures of work organizations.* Englewood Cliffs, NJ: Prentice Hall.

Walster, E., Walster, G. W., & Berscheid, E. (1978). *Equity: Theory and research.* Boston: Allyn & Bacon.

Wilpert, B. (1995). Organizational behavior. *Annual Review of Psychology, 46,* 59–90.

Wood, R. E., & Bandura, A. (1989a). Impact of conceptions of ability on self-regulatory mechanisms and complex decision making. *Journal of Personality and Social Psychology, 56,* 407–415.

Wood, R. E., & Bandura, A. (1989b). Social cognitive theory of organizational management. *Academy of Management Review, 14,* 361–384.

Wright, P. M., George, J. M., Farnsworth, S. R., & McMahan, G. C. (1993). Productivity and extra-role behavior: The effects of goals and incentives on spontaneous helping. *Journal of Applied Psychology, 78,* 374–381.

HUMAN PERFORMANCE, *10*(2), 171–192

Generalized Self-Efficacy As a Mediator and Moderator Between Control and Complexity at Work and Personal Initiative: A Longitudinal Field Study in East Germany

Christa Speier and Michael Frese
Department of Psychology
University of Giessen and University of Amsterdam

Personal initiative is one aspect of contextual performance. Combining the perspective of occupational socialization with the concept of self-efficacy, a general model is proposed and tested that views generalized work-related self-efficacy as an intervening variable in the relation between control and complexity at work and personal initiative. As part of a longitudinal study ($N = 463$ to 543) in East Germany, two different functions of self-efficacy as an intervening variable were examined: (a) self-efficacy as a mediator and (b) self-efficacy as a moderator. It was found that the relation between control and complexity and concurrent initiative is partly mediated by self-efficacy. In addition, self-efficacy functions as a moderator of the relation between control at work and retrospective initiative. Implications for the general discussion of self-efficacy and contextual performance are suggested.

Personal initiative is a behavior syndrome resulting in an individual's taking an active and self-starting approach to work and going beyond what is formally required in a given job. More specifically, personal initiative is characterized by the following aspects: (a) is consistent with the organization's mission, (b) has a long-term focus, (c) is goal oriented and action oriented, (d) is persistent in the face of barriers and setbacks, and (e) is self-starting and proactive (for a more detailed discussion of the concept, see Frese, Fay, Hilburger, Leng, & Tag, 1997; Frese, Kring, Soose, & Zempel, 1996). An individual with high personal initiative would,

Requests for reprints should be sent to Michael Frese, Department of Psychology, University of Amsterdam, Roetersstraat 15, 1018 WB Amsterdam, The Netherlands. E-mail: ao_frese@macmail.psy.uva.nl for example, look into production problems and inform the supervisor of difficulties at work.

This concept is important because it has been shown to be related to the unemployed getting a job, need for achievement, action orientation, problem- (instead of emotion-) focused coping with stress, making career plans and executing them, and wanting to be and being self-employed (Frese et al., 1997).

This article closely examines the mechanisms involved in the development of personal initiative by combining the perspective of occupational socialization (Frese, 1982) with the concept of self-efficacy (Bandura, 1977, 1986). A general model that views generalized work-related self-efficacy as an intervening variable in this socialization process is proposed and tested. Our findings should lead to a better understanding of the determinants of personal initiative that in turn may serve as the basis for practical interventions to enhance personal initiative at work.

RELATION BETWEEN CONTEXTUAL PERFORMANCE AND PERSONAL INITIATIVE

Initiative is one instance of contextual performance. Taking Borman and Motowidlo's (1993) approach as a starting point, contextual performance and personal initiative can be said to have the following points in common: (a) they do not directly relate to the technical core, (b) they are common (and equally useful) to all jobs, (c) they relate to volition, and (d) they refer to extra-role activities. Thus, the smooth functioning of the organization (Organ, 1988) is supported by contextual performance and this concept should include initiative.

Extending contextual performance to include personal initiative leads to a better and more well-rounded concept because personal initiative is an important addition to those constructs that are traditionally discussed under the rubric of contextual performance, for example, organizational citizenship behavior (OCB; Organ, 1988) or organizational spontaneity (George & Brief, 1992). First, personal initiative emphasizes the proactive nature of contextual performance. Some of the operationalizations of OCB seem to emphasize the passive and conformistic side more strongly, particularly in the factor "conformity" (Eastman, 1994).

Second, measures of contextual performance (e.g., Motowidlo & van Scotter, 1994) take the tasks at work as given at this point. Personal initiative may actually change the task itself. It may sound like a paradox that contextual performance (which is not directed to doing the task) should change the task. However, this is actually the case for OCB as well because it may lead to task enrichment. But this point has not been emphasized up to now. Thus, task changes may be an outcome of contextual performance. However, initiative is necessary to achieve these task changes.

Third, much of contextual performance has relied on supervisors' judgments. Although this is an obvious advantage to approaches that rely on one-source information typical of much of questionnaire research, there are also disadvantages. These become particularly evident when considering research on initiative. Initiative threatens the status quo (by suggesting new ways of doing things) and may, therefore, be rejected by supervisors. This point is important when doing studies in Eastern Europe because supervisors tend to be authoritarian and to punish initiative there (Schultz-Gambard & Altschuh, 1993; cf. also Pearce, Branyicki, & Bukacsi, 1994). Thus, OCB may emphasize the short-term positive social lubrication at work, whereas personal initiative aims for the long-term survival of the organization.

Fourth, by investigating initiative, it is possible to relate issues of contextual performance to entrepreneurship or intrapreneurship and thus open up an additional corpus of empirical findings of high importance (Hisrich, 1990) for the study of contextual performance.

Finally, to our knowledge, there has been no study on self-efficacy and contextual performance although self-efficacy is plausibly related to contextual performance in general and initiative in particular.

THE CONCEPT OF GENERALIZED WORK-RELATED SELF-EFFICACY

Self-efficacy is defined as "people's judgements of their capabilities to organize and execute courses of action required to attain designated types of performances" (Bandura, 1986, p. 391). Bandura suggests that self-efficacy has an important impact on human action and performance. It determines the initial decision to perform a behavior, the effort expended, and the persistence in the face of obstacles. Empirical studies have established a relation between self-efficacy and a wide range of human behaviors (e.g., Barling & Beattie, 1983; Stumpf, Brief, & Hartman, 1987; Taylor, Locke, Lee, & Gist, 1984). A recent meta-analysis (Sadri & Robertson, 1993) showed that self-efficacy is positively related both to performance and to choice of behavior in the context of organizational behavior.

Self-efficacy varies in generality (Bandura, 1986). As Bandura stated, "people may judge themselves efficacious only in certain domains of functioning or across a wide range of activities and situations" (Bandura, 1986, p. 396). Despite Bandura's emphasis on high specificity and high malleability of self-efficacy, we see self-efficacy within the wider concept of Rotter's (1966, 1975) generalized beliefs that Rotter used as a conceptualization of personality variables (cf. Eden & Kinnar, 1991). Two reasons speak for a conceptualization of generalized self-efficacy when predicting initiative. First, following Rotter's argument (1966, 1975), generalized expectations have an impact on behavior, especially in new and ambiguous situations. Because personal initiative implies that one acts in new and ambiguous situations, generalized expectations are of particular importance here. Second, it follows from the perspective of occupational socialization that the effects of work conditions tend to generalize from the original situation (e.g., Kohn & Schooler, 1982). For example, if the work situation provides opportunities to work on challenging tasks, a person does not only learn that he or she can master these specific tasks, but, additionally, should develop a more general sense of mastery, that is, generalized self-efficacy.

Our study was concerned with personal initiative at work; therefore, self-efficacy was conceptualized as generalized work-related expectation. Thus, our concept is on a medium level of generality that is between a specific concept, for example, of asking whether or not one is able to do a certain task, and a highly generalized concept, for example, asking whether or not one has the capabilities to handle difficult job situations in general. Our concept of work-related generalized self-efficacy should correlate with highly generalized self-efficacy expectations. It should also be related to work-related self-esteem, because self-esteem is a general evaluation of one's own competencies to deal with work (Gist & Mitchell, 1992; Mohr, 1986).

Although there is a relation between the two constructs of self-efficacy and optimism, they should not be confused. Optimism refers to positive thinking, that is, the belief that one will generally experience good outcomes in life (Scheier & Carver, 1985). Thus, this concept does not presuppose that one has to be active to bring about the positive events. Self-efficacy, on the other hand, refers to the notion that one can bring about positive results through one's own actions. Because both optimism and self-efficacy (at least implicitly) refer to positive outcomes, there should be some relation between optimism and self-efficacy. But because the process by which this positive outcome is achieved is different, the correlation between measures of these two constructs should not be high.

SELF-EFFICACY AND PERSONAL INITIATIVE

Because personal initiative refers to complex actions that are difficult to maintain despite obstacles, it can be hypothesized that self-efficacy is important for personal initiative. This is so because self-efficacy helps to increase the probability of performing a difficult action and increases the effort and persistence to pursue this action. Conversely, low self-efficacy should impede personal initiative because low self-efficacious individuals tend to avoid challenging situations and to give up quickly in the face of obstacles.

CONTROL AND COMPLEXITY AT WORK AND SELF-EFFICACY

People in East Germany are often said to show less personal initiative and self-efficacy than people in West Germany. Frese, Kring, et al. (1996) found empirical evidence for this hypothesis. Their findings suggest that this difference between East and West Germany is mainly due to occupational socialization effects, with control and complexity at work being important in this socialization process.

Bandura (1986) proposed that self-efficacy is developed throughout a person's learning history. He described four broad sources of information involved in the development of self-efficacy: enactive mastery, vicarious experience, verbal persuasion, and physiological arousal, with enactive mastery being the most important one. In the work context, enactive mastery can be experienced when one is able to make decisions, to work on challenging tasks, and to make use of one's competencies. Within the concept of occupational socialization (Frese, 1982), enactive mastery implies that there are work conditions that lead to the development of self-efficacy. The most important work conditions are control and complexity at work. Control implies that important decisions can be made by the incumbent. Complexity means performing challenging tasks (Frese, 1989). If control at work is low (nearly every step at work is prescribed), doing the task provides little information about one's personal effectiveness. Thus, there are few mastery experiences, and, consequently, few opportunities for developing self-efficacy. Complex tasks provide opportunities to apply individual skills and knowledge, thus also serving as a source of experiences relevant for self-efficacy. It follows that both control and complexity at work should have an impact on self-efficacy.

A GENERAL MODEL OF THE RELATION BETWEEN CONTROL AND COMPLEXITY AND PERSONAL INITIATIVE: SELF-EFFICACY AS AN INTERVENING VARIABLE

A general model that combines the expected relations between control and complexity, self-efficacy, and personal initiative at work is presented in Figure 1. Self-efficacy is conceptualized as an intervening variable in the relation between control and complexity as predictors and personal initiative at work as criterion. Mediator and moderator functions of an intervening variable may be differentiated (Frese, 1985; James & Brett, 1984).

The mediator function of self-efficacy links the work situation to personal initiative (see "a" in Figure 1). Such a relation implies that control and complexity have a direct effect on self-efficacy, and self-efficacy has a direct effect on personal initiative. Thus, control and complexity have an impact on personal initiative because they help to increase self-efficacy. They provide for mastery experiences and thus lead to a higher degree of generalized self-efficacy that, in turn, leads to higher personal initiative.

Longitudinally, two varieties of the mediator effect are plausible. First, control and complexity at work may have a concurrent effect on self-efficacy, and,

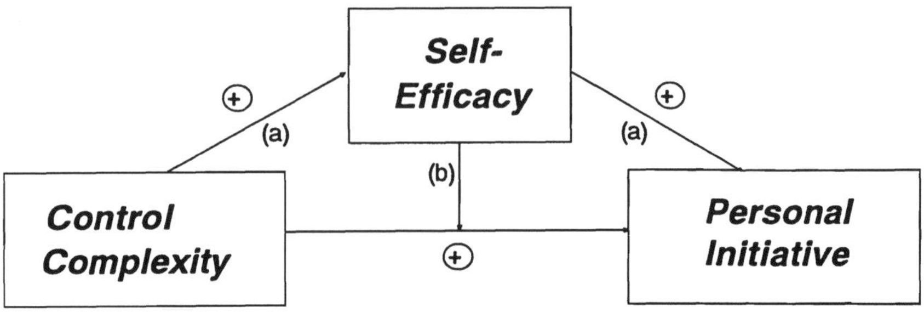

FIGURE 1 Hypothetical relations between control and complexity, self-efficacy, and personal initiative. This is a simplified model not including possible feedback loops. Note that the relations among the constructs may also be reciprocal over time.

subsequently, self-efficacy leads to changes in later personal initiative (*concurrent mediator model*). Second, the work conditions may need some time to develop their influence on self-efficacy later on, and self-efficacy, once it is increased, leads to more personal initiative concurrently (*lagged mediator model*). From the perspective of occupational socialization we prefer the lagged mediator model, supposing that control and complexity at work have to exist for some time to influence self-efficacy, and that self-efficacy, once it has been changed, is translated into action without much delay.

Additionally, self-efficacy may function as a moderator (see "b" in Figure 1). According to the moderator model the relation between work conditions and personal initiative should be a function of the level of self-efficacy. Individuals with high self-efficacy may compensate for a lack of control and complexity because they will assume to be able to influence things despite the lack of situational support. Thus, they will show personal initiative despite situational constraints. On the other hand, low self-efficacious people may give up quickly if the situation is not conducive to show initiative. However, they will show a high degree of initiative if the situation provides enough opportunities to make initiative easy. This moderator effect implies that control and complexity should have a stronger impact on personal initiative for people having low self-efficacy than for highly self-efficacious individuals.

Similar to the mediator effects discussed earlier, two models of a moderator effect are plausible: the concurrent moderator model with earlier self-efficacy functioning as moderator, and the lagged moderator model with later self-efficacy being the moderator. In contrast to the mediator hypothesis, the concurrent multiplicative effect of earlier control and complexity and earlier self-efficacy on later personal initiative is expected here because there should be a compensatory relations between concurrently appearing work conditions and self-efficacy.

A particular variable may function both as a mediator and as a moderator in the same model (James & Brett, 1984). The following analyses will determine whether and to what degree self-efficacy functions as mediator and/or moderator.

METHOD

Participants

The data reported in this article were part of a larger longitudinal study starting in July 1990 (other results on East–West differences were reported in Frese, Kring, et al., 1996, and on validity and reliability in Frese et al., 1997). A representative sample was drawn from Dresden, a large city in East Germany. It is the capital of Saxonia and, compared to other cities in East Germany, it is relatively wealthy. The selection of participants was done by randomly selecting streets, selecting every third house on a street, and within each house every fourth party (in smaller houses every third party was chosen). All people between the ages of 18 and 65 with full-time employment were asked to participate in a 1-hr interview and to fill out a questionnaire. The refusal rate of 33% was quite low for this type of study.

Because personal initiative was fully measured only in Waves 3 and 4, we concentrate on these two times. At t3 (August 1991), the sample consisted of 543 people and at t4 (September 1992) it consisted of 506 people. Experimental mortality was not found to change the characteristics of the sample substantially.[1] Only people who were employed at t3 were included because no measures of initiative in current work conditions were available for the unemployed. Thus, the sample analyzed here consisted of 363 persons. Forty-eight percent of the participants were women and 52% were men. The mean age of participants was 40.5 years (SD = 11.3 years).

Because of missing data, the sample size varies across the analyses. Pairwise deletion of cases was used in the correlational and regression analyses because it has been demonstrated to be the best procedure for handling missing data (Roth, Switzer, Campion, & Jones, 1994).

---

[1]To compare the drop-outs from t1 to t4 with full participants, 16 two-tailed t tests for independent samples were computed for all the variables discussed in this article including the potential covariates. Because a multiple t test is a conservative test when used in this way, a Bonferroni-adjusted alpha of .05/16 = .0031 was used (Miller, 1966). No significant differences were found for the variables discussed in this article, except for optimism for better work, where the drop-outs reported a higher level of optimism.

Measures

The data were collected by either a standardized interview or a questionnaire. The interviews were carried out by trained interviewers. All of the interviewers' codings were re-rated by a second judge. The codings were culturally cross-checked, that is, interviewers from East Germany were re-raters of those interviews coded from Western interviewers and vice versa (for a detailed description of the interview procedures, cf. Frese et al., 1997). Means, standard deviations, reliabilities, and intercorrelations of all of the scales are reported in Table 1.

Work conditions. Control at work and complexity of work were measured with questionnaire scales developed by Semmer (1984; adaptation by Zapf, 1991; range from 1 to 7). *Control at work* consists of four Likert items measuring job discretion in the work place, for example "Can you decide on your own how to carry out your work?" *Complexity of work* is also composed of four Likert items referring to the difficulty of the work task, for example, "Do you get special tasks that are unusual and exceptionally difficult?" Semmer and Dunckel (1991) reported correlations of .50 and .54 respectively between measures provided by the participants and observations done by trained observers in a sample of factory workers.

Self-efficacy. Because our study is concerned with personal initiative at work, self-efficacy should be measured as a generalized work-related expectation. To our knowledge, no such scale has been developed before (cf. however, Saks, 1995). Therefore, a new six-item Likert scale was developed for this study (each with a range of 1 to 5, the scale divided by the number of items). In Table 2 the items and their item-total correlations are presented.[2] Cronbach's alphas were .68 (t3) and .67 (t4). Test–retest correlation was $r_{t3/t4} = .69$. Thus, work-related self-efficacy is a relatively stable construct.

The construct validity of the newly developed scale was assessed by correlating our measure of self-efficacy with related personality characteristics. We assumed that our measure of self-efficacy should be related to a highly generalized measure of self-efficacy, work-related self-esteem, control cognitions, and certain forms of optimism. These constructs were operationalized by using a measure of generalized self-efficacy that was not work-related (Schwarzer, Bäßler, Kwiatek, Schröder & Zhang, 1997), work-related self-esteem (Mohr, 1986), individual and collective control cognitions (Frese, 1986), general optimism (Scheier & Carver, 1985), and four measures of specific optimism that were developed for this study (optimism

[2]Compared to earlier versions of the self-efficacy scale, one item was replaced because of a certain overlap with personal initiative.

TABLE 1
Means, Standard Deviations, Reliabilities, and Intercorrelations for the Main Variables

Variable	*M*	*SD*	*1*	*2*	*3*	*4*	*5*	*6*	*7*	*8*
Control at work$_{t3}$	3.55	0.82	(.77)							
Complexity of work$_{t3}$	3.44	0.76	.46**	(.66)						
Self-efficacy$_{t3}$	3.46	0.51	.22**	.14**	(.68)					
Self-efficacy$_{t4}$	3.49	0.49	.20**	.19**	.69**	(.67)				
Initiative-Retro$_{t3}$[a]	0.12	1.66	.23**	.28**	.09*	.14**	(.78)			
Initiative-Retro$_{t4}$[a]	–0.02	1.66	.25**	.25**	.06	.14**	.49**	(.84)		
Initiative-Conc$_{t3}$[a]	0.17	3.07	.21**	.30**	.14**	.14**	.47**	.38**	(.79)[b]	
Initiative-Conc$_{t4}$[a]	0.26	2.90	.29**	.31**	.18**	.18**	.46**	.49**	.56**	(.74)[b]

Note. n = 312 to 363; variation is due to missing data. Values in parentheses are reliability coefficients for the full sample (Cronbach's Alpha). Means, standard deviations, and correlations were calculated for the subsample analyzed in this article. Retro = retrospective; Conc = concurrent.

[a]Sum of z scores. [b]Cronbach's Alpha based on scales.

$*p < .05$. $**p < .01$.

TABLE 2
Means, Standard Deviations, and Item-Total Correlations of the Work-Related Self-Efficacy Scale (t3)

Item	*M*	*SD*	$R_{it\text{-}i}$
When I am confronted with a new task, I am often afraid of not being able to handle it.[a]	3.61	.83	.37
I judge my abilities to be high.	3.27	.71	.44
If I want to achieve something, I can overcome setbacks without giving up my goal.	3.63	.82	.49
When I want to reach a goal, I am usually able to succeed.	3.68	.70	.46
In case of becoming unemployed, I am convinced that, because of my abilities, I will soon find a new job.	3.07	1.05	.38
If I had to change my job, I am sure I would be up to the demands.	3.40	.81	.40

[a]Item inverted.

for better work, for minimizing the effects of unemployment, for better economies, for more leisure time).

Table 3 shows that our theoretical expectations were met. Work-related self-efficacy correlated positively with a non-work oriented measure of generalized self-efficacy, self-esteem, individual and collective control cognitions, and general optimism. For the different measures of specific optimism, correlations with self-efficacy were stronger when the measure of optimism was related to the work situation. Thus, our measure is of medium generality—more specific than generalized self-efficacy (Schwarzer et al., 1997), but also generalized with regard to various work situations.

In summary, correlations with other constructs provide evidence for construct validity of the work-related self-efficacy scale. Additionally, the correlations were not overly high, indicating that the instrument measures a construct distinct from the other personality measures.

Personal initiative. Personal initiative was operationalized as described by Frese, Kring, et al. (1996; Frese et al., 1997) with a combination of several indicators developed from interview material. Two broad factors were built by summing up the *z* scores of the indicators.

The first factor, retrospective initiative, covers two aspects of retrospectively reported initiative at work. It consists of two scales, initiative at work and initiative with regard to colleagues. Memory factors are more important here than in the second factor.

TABLE 3
Correlations of Work-Related Self-Efficacy With Other Constructs (All t3)

Variable	*Work-Related Self-Efficacy*
Non-work generalized self-efficacy[a]	.53*
Work-related self-esteem	.52*
Control cognitions	
Individual	.28*
Collective	.22*
Optimism	
Optimism general	.38*
Optimism better work	.23*
Optimism unemployment	.35*
Optimism leisure time	.02

[a]This correlation refers to another measurement wave because generalized self-efficacy was not measured at t3 and t4.
*$p < .01$.

Initiative at work was measured by asking the participants about four different activities at work during the last year, for example, whether they had provided a suggestion that led to an improvement in the work process. If the answer was positive, the interviewer probed for what kind of suggestion it was, whether it was the participant's own idea, how often it was done, whether people in that kind of job would typically do these things, and so forth. After the session, the interviewer judged whether the participant's behavior constituted something that went beyond the duties of the job and rated the amount of initiative demonstrated on a 5-point scale. The interrater correlation was $r = .84$ (t3).

In addition to the work-related questions, three questions were asked about initiative with regard to colleagues, for example, whether or not the participant had been active in defending a colleague's rights. These questions were treated in the same way as initiative at work. The interrater correlation was $r = .79$, (t3).

The second factor, concurrent initiative, consists of four scales and is concerned mainly with initiative shown in the context of the interview. Education initiative is an index built from five interview ratings, for example, whether the participant intends to participate in some continuing education in the future. The interrater agreement was $r = .88$ (t3).

Interviewer evaluation consists of 11 Likert items asking the interviewers for their subjective impression of how proactive the participants were (no re-rating was done here because it was based on a subjective impression).

Overcoming barriers measured the tenacity and creativity in solving problems. It was inspired by the situational interview (Latham & Saari, 1984). The interviewer presented four problems; for example, what the participant would do if he or she was fired from a job. After the participants' response the interviewer told the participant that this strategy would not work and asked the participant to think of additional strategies (three times). Thus, each time the interviewer suggested that the strategy was not good enough yet, it was measured how many barriers the participant was able to overcome. The interrater agreement was $r = .80$ (t3).

Active approach measured the way the participants approached the barriers in the situational interview. If they were delegating the solutions to someone else (e.g., the supervisor), this was seen as less active than when they were trying to actively solve the problem themselves (interviewer's rating, no interrater reliability computed).

RESULTS

Self-Efficacy as a Mediator

According to the mediator model the following relations between control and complexity, self-efficacy, and personal initiative were expected: positive correlations between control and complexity and self-efficacy, between self-efficacy and personal initiative, and between control and complexity and personal initiative. Additionally, the correlation between control and complexity and personal initiative should be reduced when the mediator self-efficacy is held constant with a partial correlation procedure.

The bivariate relations between the three sets of variables were mainly in the expected direction (see Table 1). Self-efficacy correlated moderately positive with control at work and complexity of work (*r*s between .14 and .22, all *p*s < .01). Control and complexity correlated significantly with personal initiative (*r*s between .21 and .31). Self-efficacy correlated significantly with personal initiative (*r*s between .09 and .18), except for the correlation of self-efficacy$_{t3}$ with retrospective initiative$_{t4}$, that did not reach significance.

These significant bivariate relations reported so far are necessary, but not sufficient, conditions for the validity of the mediator model. Hierarchical regression analyses (Cohen & Cohen, 1975) were used to examine whether the relation between control and complexity and personal initiative was actually mediated by self-efficacy (cf. Tables 4 and 5). In these analyses, prior initiative values (t3) were always entered in the first block together with age, sex, and qualification as potential confounding variables, so that changes in personal initiative were analyzed. This procedure generally leads to small relationships, because prior change in personal initiative is also partialled out.

The following regression analyses were computed. First, the nonmediator model was tested by regressing personal initiative (t4) on control and complexity (t3) to verify which amount of variance in the change of personal initiative is explained by the work conditions (Analysis 1). Second, personal initiative (t4) was regressed

TABLE 4
Mediator Model: Multiple Regression of Concurrent Initiative on Control and Complexity and Self-Efficacy

Predictor	R^2	R^2_{inc}	R^2_{diff}	R^2_{red}	*B*
Nonmediator model					
Step 1	.41***	.41***			
Initiative-Conc$_{t3}$					.31***
Initiative-Retro$_{t3}$					.46***
Qualification$_{t3}$					.76***
Sex					.44*
Age					–.03**
Step 2	.43***	.02**			
Control$_{t3}$					.34*
Complexity$_{t3}$					.24
Concurrent mediator model[a]					
Step 2	.42***	.01***			
Self-efficacy$_{t3}$					.68***
Step 3	.44***	.01***	.01	50%	
Control$_{t3}$					.26
Complexity$_{t3}$					.24
Lagged mediator model[a]					
Step 2	.42***	.01**			
Self-efficacy$_{t4}$					.62**
Step 3	.43**	.01**	.01	50%	
Control$_{t3}$					.30
Complexity$_{t3}$					.22

Note. Retro = retrospective; Conc = concurrent.
[a]Step 1 is identical for all three models.
**p* < .10. ***p* < .05. ****p* < .01.

on self-efficacy (t3) and control and complexity (t3), entering self-efficacy in the second and control and complexity in the third block (Analysis 2: concurrent mediator model). This computes the amount of variance in the change of personal initiative being accounted for by the work conditions after controlling for the effects of self-efficacy (t3). Third, the lagged mediator model was tested in a similar way by regressing change in personal initiative on self-efficacy (t4) and control and complexity (t3), again entering self-efficacy in the second and control and complexity in the third step (Analysis 3). In each case, the R^2 difference between mediator model and the nonmediator model is displayed in the third column in Table 4 and Table 5 (the percentage of the R^2 reduction is shown in the fourth column).

For concurrent initiative (see Table 4), regressing changes in personal initiative on control and complexity resulted in $R^2_{\text{inc}} = .02$ ($p < .01$) for the nonmediator model

TABLE 5
Mediator Model: Multiple Regression of Retrospective Initiative on Control and Complexity and Self-Efficacy

Predictor	R^2	R^2_{inc}	R^2_{diff}	R^2_{red}	B
Nonmediator model					
Step 1	.29***	.29***			
Initiative-Retro$_{t3}$					.41***
Initiative-Conc$_{t3}$					.05
Qualification$_{t3}$					.36***
Sex					.07
Age					–.01
Step 2	.30***	.01			
Control$_{t3}$					.20*
Complexity$_{t3}$					.03
Concurrent mediator model[a]					
Step 2	.29***	.00			
Self-efficacy$_{t3}$					.00
Step 3	.30***	.01	.00	0%	
Control$_{t3}$					.21*
Complexity$_{t3}$					.03
Lagged mediator model[a]					
Step 2	.29***	.00			
Self-efficacy$_{t4}$					.18
Step 3	.30**	.01	.00	0%	
Control$_{t3}$					.20*
Complexity$_{t3}$					.02

Note. Retro = retrospective; Conc = concurrent.
[a]Step 1 is identical for all three models.
$*p < .10$. $**p < .05$. $***p < .01$.

(Analysis 1). Thus, the work conditions predicted changes in initiative—a confirmation of the occupational socialization perspective. Entering self-efficacy (t3) in the second block (Analysis 2: concurrent mediator model) resulted in R^2inc = .01 ($p < .01$), indicating that self-efficacy, too, significantly predicted changes in initiative. The amount of variance accounted for by control and complexity was reduced to $R^2_{\text{inc}} = .01$ ($p < .05$), indicating that 50% of the common variance of control and complexity and the change in concurrent initiative was mediated by self-efficacy (t3). The same pattern was observed for the lagged mediator model. Thus, for concurrent initiative, both mediator models were supported by our data. Control and complexity were shown to have both direct and indirect effects on concurrent initiative.

In contrast to concurrent initiative, neither control and complexity nor self-efficacy significantly predicted changes in retrospective initiative (see Table 5). Thus, both the occupational socialization perspective and the mediator model were not supported for retrospective initiative.

Self-Efficacy as a Moderator

The moderator hypotheses were tested by moderated regression analyses (Stone & Hollenbeck, 1984; Zedeck, 1971). Separate moderator analyses were performed for the two criterion variables, concurrent and retrospective initiative, and for the concurrent and lagged moderator model. In the first step, personal initiative (t3), the covariates, and all main effects, that is, control at work, complexity of work, and self-efficacy (t3 and t4), were entered into the equation. In the second step, all interaction terms were entered into the equation. Because moderator effects are difficult to detect in field studies (McClelland & Judd, 1993), and because we

TABLE 6
Moderator Model: Hierarchical Regression Analysis on Retrospective Initiative (t4)

Predictor	R^2	R^2_{inc}	*B*
Step 1: Main effects[a]	30***	.30***	
Step 2: Concurrent moderator model	.31***	.01	
Control at Work$_{t3}$ × Self-efficacy$_{t3}$			–.43*
Complexity of Work$_{t3}$ × Self-efficacy$_{t3}$			.20
Step 2: Lagged moderator model	.32***	.02**	
Control at Work$_{t3}$ × Self-efficacy$_{t4}$			–.57**
Complexity of Work$_{t3}$ × Self-efficacy$_{t4}$			–.04

[a]Main effects were initiative$_{t3}$, qualification$_{t3}$, sex, age, control at work$_{t3}$, complexity of work$_{t3}$, self-efficacy$_{t3}$, and self-efficacy$_{t4}$.
*$p < .10$. **$p < .05$. ***$p < .01$.

TABLE 7
Moderator Model: Hierarchical Regression Analysis on Concurrent Initiative (t4)

Predictor	R^2	R^2_{inc}	*B*
Step 1: Main effects[a]	.44*	.44*	
Step 2: Concurrent moderator model	.44*	.01	
Control at Work$_{t3}$ × Self-efficacy$_{t3}$			.67
Complexity of Work$_{t3}$ × Self-efficacy$_{t3}$			– .09
Step 2: Lagged moderator model	.44*	.00	
Control at Work$_{t3}$ × Self-efficacy$_{t4}$			–.07
Complexity of Work$_{t3}$ × Self-efficacy$_{t4}$			–.40

[a]Main effects were initiative$_{t3}$, qualification$_{t3}$, sex, age, control at work$_{t3}$, complexity of work$_{t3}$, self-efficacy$_{t3}$, and self-efficacy$_{t4}$.
*$p < .01$.

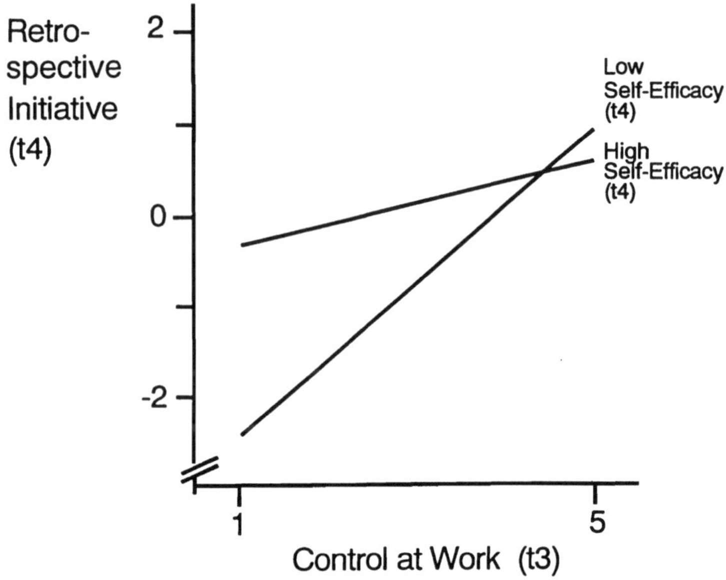

FIGURE 2 Lagged moderator effect of self-efficacy on the relation between control at work and retrospective initiative.

wanted to avoid a Type II error due to lack of power, we also calculated the significance level of .10 (as was done, e.g., by LaRocco, House, & French, 1980).

The results of the regression analyses are presented in Table 6 and Table 7. For retrospective initiative (see Table 6), all main effects entered in the first step accounted for 30% of the variance in the criterion. This step was identical for both the concurrent and the lagged moderator model. Entering the interaction terms did not lead to a significant increase of criterion variance for the concurrent moderator model, but for the lagged moderator model an additional 2% of the variance in retrospective initiative was explained, with Control at Work × Self-Efficacy$_{t4}$ showing a significant negative regression coefficient (B = –.57, p < .01). This negative B indicates that high self-efficacy decreased the relation between retrospective initiative and control at work.

Figure 2 depicts the moderator effect of self-efficacy and control at work by showing two regression lines for the regression of retrospective initiative (t4) on control at work (t3), one for the high and one for the low self-efficacy subgroups.[3] As expected, the relation between control at work and retrospective initiative was stronger for people with low self-efficacy than for those with high self-efficacy.

[3]The high and low subsamples contained all participants with self-efficacy scores at least 1 standard deviation above and below the mean.

Although the low self-efficacious individuals reported as much initiative as the high self-efficacious individuals under work conditions providing high control, there was a clear-cut difference under low control conditions. Here, the low self-efficacious revealed only a small amount of retrospective initiative compared to the high self-efficacious.

The results for concurrent initiative are presented in Table 7. Here, the main effects accounted for 44% of the variance in concurrent initiative. Entering the interaction terms did not lead to a significant increase in the criterion for both the concurrent and the lagged moderator model. Thus, the moderator model was not supported for concurrent initiative.

DISCUSSION

This study has looked at one issue of contextual performance, initiative, and has attempted to combine the perspective of occupational socialization (Frese, 1982) with Bandura's (1977, 1986) concept of self-efficacy. Both the mediator and moderator functions were partly supported in this study.

The results confirm the mediating effect of self-efficacy in the relation between control and complexity at work and concurrent initiative. Half of the common variance of control and complexity and later concurrent initiative was found to be mediated by self-efficacy. Thus, control and complexity have their effect on concurrent initiative partly via self-efficacy. The longitudinal design of the study and keeping the stability of initiative constant allows the interpretation that the mediator affects changes in personal initiative.

One can differentiate between a full and a partial mediation model (James & Brett, 1984). A full model would imply that there is no other variable mediating between the work conditions and initiative. Such a full mediation model was not supported by our data. The model supported here can be best described as partial mediation, that is, only a part of the total effect of control and complexity on concurrent initiative is due to mediation by self-efficacy. This is not surprising, because control and complexity are thought to have a direct activating effect as well (e.g., Karasek & Theorell, 1990). In addition, other variables may function as mediators in the relation between control and complexity and personal initiative, for example, control cognitions (Frese, 1986), readiness to change at work (Frese & Plüddemann, 1993), and control rejection (Frese, Erbe-Heinbokel, Grefe, Rybowiak, & Weike, 1994).

Our results are in line with other studies. Self-efficacy has also been shown to be of high importance in another study on one instance of initiative—namely submitting suggestions to the company to improve efficiency and working conditions (Frese, Teng, & Wijnen, 1996). This study looked at blue collar workers in a Dutch company and thus provides a reinforcement of these results in another culture and within a different setting.

Self-efficacy was also found to moderate the relation between control at work and the development of retrospective initiative. As expected, there was a stronger impact of control at work on initiative in people with low self-efficacy than in those with high self-efficacy for retrospective initiative. This implies that highly self-efficacious individuals are less dependent on the external work conditions than the low self-efficacious in the development of retrospective initiative. Their high self-efficacy shields them from the impact of low control at work. This corresponds with the experimental findings by Jerusalem and Schwarzer (1992), who showed that high self-efficacious individuals were less affected by stressful situations than individuals with low self-efficacy. In terms of personality effects at work, personality (self-efficacy) plays a role mainly in the low control condition. In terms of work conditions, control is important mainly in people with low self-efficacy (cf. Adler, 1994). Saks (1995) also put self-efficacy within the context of an occupational socialization perspective with adjustment as the dependent variable. This study provided only limited support for a mediation hypothesis. However, there were moderator effects of self-efficacy and training. They also support a compensation effect. People with low self-efficacy profit more from training than people with high self-efficacy.

Our data have implications for the general discussion of self-efficacy. For example, Gist and Mitchell (1992) argued that there is a direct concurrent effect of work conditions on self-efficacy judgments. Although we do not generally disagree with their approach, our results only partly support their hypothesis: Both concurrent and lagged mediator models are supported by the data presented here.

For contextual performance, the following conclusions are important. First, one aspect of contextual performance—personal initiative—was researched that emphasizes the active nature of dealing with work life. Second, the notion of occupational socialization should be emphasized more strongly in contextual performance. Although George and Brief (1992) suggested that we look at direct precursors (e.g., positive mood) of helping behavior, it may pay to look at the long-term development of contextual performance at work as well. Control and complexity are important starting points. Other aspects of socialization come readily to mind, for example, mentor systems, socialization practices that reduce the self-confidence of the newcomers, and so forth (cf. van Maanen & Schein, 1979). Third, we suggest that self-efficacy may well be important for other areas of contextual performance as well. If a person does not think that he or she can actually do well in helping others, he or she will probably not do it. Fourth, our contribution has been to look at an interesting sample and to look at it from a longitudinal perspective. Finally, we think that personality factors are probably good predictors of initiative, as they are for contextual performance in general (Borman & Motowidlo, 1993). However, we assume that different personality dimensions will predict initiative than OCB. For example, we have shown that initiative does not correlate highly with job satisfaction (Frese et al., 1997), although it does correlate highly with OCB (Organ, 1988).

A number of methodological issues of the study need to be discussed. First, one initiative variable—retrospective initiative—required participants to recall past behavior. Although care was taken by the interviewers to distinguish fact from fiction, this variable has to be interpreted more cautiously than concurrent initiative. Memory effects have been shown to be important in retrospective reports (Neisser, 1982).

Our measure of work-related self-efficacy should be improved. Although its reliability is higher than .60 and, therefore, adequate for early stages of research (Nunnally, 1978), its reliability is at the lower end for practical purposes.

It might be argued that the effects reported here are quite small. However, for several reasons we think that they should be taken seriously. First, we have used conservative methodologies like moderated regression analyses and partialling out the stabilities of the dependent variables and possible covariates. Partialling out the stabilities and covariates decreases the amount of variance that can be explained by the predictors. Moreover, the potential impact of earlier self-efficacy on initiative at t3 is also removed by this approach. Second, there is no common method variance between the predictor variables and the criterion because the predictors have been measured with questionnaires and the initiative variables with standardized interviews. Thus, all the effects reported here are probably at the lower boundary of the actual relations. Finally, it has been shown by several authors that even small correlations can be of high practical relevance (e.g., Abelson, 1985; Frese, 1985).

There may be some practical implications of the results of our study. A starting point for interventions may be to increase personal initiative by making control and complexity available in the work situation (e.g., Hackman & Oldham, 1980). A second issue is to train self-efficacy to increase personal initiative. Because self-efficacy changes are mainly based on enactive mastery (Bandura, 1986), training should provide those experiences.

ACKNOWLEDGMENTS

The project AHUS (*A*ktives *H*andeln in einer *U*mbruchsituation—Active Actions in a Radical Change Situation) is supported by the Deutsche Forschungsgemeinschaft (DFG, No Fr 638/6–5; principal investigator, Michael Frese).

Thanks are also due to Hypo-Bank and Tobacco Reynolds, as well as the "Hundertjahre Stiftung" of the University of Munich. Members of the project have been and are: D. Fay, H. Garst, S. Hilligloh, C. Speier, and T. Wagner; student members were C. Dormann, M. Erbe-Heinbokel, T. Hillburger, J. Grefe, M. Krachelctz, K. Leng, K. Plüddemann, V. Rybowiak, A. Weike (Giessen), R. Bamesberger, A. Dehnelt, G. Engstle, M. Fontin, B. Hartmann, J. Haushofer, B. Immler, E. Kahl, M. Eichholz, S. Kemmler, C. Lamberts, R. Lautner, A. Röver, B. Schier, S. Schmider, D. Schweighart, H. Simon, B. Waldhauser, T. Weber, and B. Winkler (Munich).

For constructive criticism we would like to thank Felix Brodbeck, Doris Fay, Jerilyn Lewter, and Sabine Sonnentag.

REFERENCES

Abelson, R. P. (1985). A variance explanation paradox: When a little is a lot. *Psychological Bulletin, 97,* 129–133.

Adler, S. (1994, August). *Personality and work behavior: Exploring the linkages.* Paper presented at the 23rd International Congress of Applied Psychology, Madrid.

Bandura, A. (1977). Self-efficacy: Towards a unifying theory of behavioral change. *Psychological Review, 84,* 191–215.

Bandura, A. (1986). *Social foundations of thought and action.* Englewood Cliffs, NJ: Prentice Hall.

Barling, J., & Beattie, R. (1983). Self-efficacy beliefs and sales performance. *Journal of Organizational Behavior Management, 5,* 41–51.

Borman, W. C., & Motowidlo, S. J. (1993). Expanding the criterion domain to include elements of contextual performance. In N. Schmitt & W. C. Borman (Eds.), *Personnel selection in organizations* (pp. 71–98). San Francisco: Jossey-Bass.

Cohen, J., & Cohen, P. (1975). *Applied multiple regression/correlation analysis for the behavioral sciences.* Hillsdale, NJ: Lawrence Erlbaum Associates, Inc.

Eastman, K. K. (1994). In the eyes of the beholder: An attributional approach to ingratiation and organizational citizenship behavior. *Academy of Management Journal, 37,* 1397–1391.

Eden, D., & Kinnar, J., (1991). Modeling Galatea: Boosting self-efficacy to increase volunteering. *Journal of Applied Psychology, 76,* 770–780.

Frese, M. (1982). Occupational socialization and psychological development: An underemphasized research perspective in industrial psychology. *Journal of Occupational Psychology, 55,* 209–224.

Frese, M. (1985). Stress at work and psychosomatic complaints: A causal interpretation. *Journal of Applied Psychology, 70,* 314–328.

Frese, M. (1986). *Abschlußbericht, Deutsche Forschungsgemeinschaft: Soziale Unterstützung, Kontrollüberzeugungen, Coping und Abwehr als intervenierende Variablen des Zusammenhangs von Streß am Arbeitsplatz und psychosomatischen Beschwerden* [Final report for the German Research Foundation: Social support, control beliefs, coping, and defense as intervening variables in the relationship between stress in the workplace and psychosomatic complaints]. Munich, Germany: University of Munich.

Frese, M. (1989). Theoretical models of control and health. In S. L. Sauter, J. J. Hurrell, & C. L. Cooper (Eds.), *Job control and worker health* (pp. 107–128). London: Wiley.

Frese, M., Erbe-Heinbokel, M., Grefe, J., Rybowiak, V., & Weike, A. (1994). "Mir ist es lieber, wenn ich genau gesagt bekomme, was ich zu tun habe."—Probleme der Akzeptanz von Verantwortung und von Handlungsspielräumen in Ost und West ["I prefer being told exactly what to do." Problems of accepting responsibility and control at work in the East and West]. *Zeitschrift für Arbeits-und Organisationspsychologie, 38,* 22–33.

Frese, M., Fay, D., Hilburger, T., Leng, K., & Tag, A. (1997). The concept of personal initiative: Operationalization, reliability and validity in two German samples. *Journal of Occupational and Organizational Psychology, 70.*

Frese, M., Kring, W., Soose, A., & Zempel, J. (1996). Personal initiative at work: Differences between East and West-Germany. *Academy of Management Journal, 39,* 37–63.

Frese, M., & Plüddemann, K. (1993). Umstellungsbereitschaft im Osten und Westen Deutschlands: Inflexibilität als Gefahrenzeichen? [Readiness to change in East and West Germany: Inflexibility as a danger signal?] *Zeitschrift für Sozialpsychologie, 24,* 198–210.

Frese, M., Teng, E., & Wijnen, C. J. D. (1996). *Helping to improve suggestion systems: Psychological predictors of giving suggestions in a Dutch company.* Manuscript submitted for publication, University of Amsterdam.

George, J. M., & Brief, A. P. 1992. Feeling good-doing good: A conceptual analysis of the mood at work-organizational spontaneity relationship. *Psychological Bulletin, 112,* 310–329.

Gist, M. E., & Mitchell, T. R. (1992). Self-efficacy: A theoretical analysis of its determinants and malleability. *Academy of Management Review, 17,* 183–211.

Hackman, J. R., & Oldham, G. (1980). *Work redesign.* Reading, MA: Addison-Wesley.

Hisrich, R. D. (1990). Entrepreneurship/intrapreneurship. *American Psychologist, 45,* 209–222.

James, L. R., & Brett, J. M. (1984). Mediators, moderators and tests for mediation. *Journal of Applied Psychology, 69,* 307–321.

Jerusalem, M., & Schwarzer, R. (1992). Self-efficacy as a resource factor in stress appraisal processes. In R. Schwarzer (Ed.), *Self-efficacy: Thought control of action* (pp. 195–213). Washington, DC: Hemisphere Publishing Corporation.

Karasek, R., & Theorell, T. (1990). *Healthy work: Stress, productivity, and the reconstruction of working life.* New York: Free Press.

Kohn, M. L., & Schooler, C. (1982). Job conditions and personality: A longitudinal assessment of their reciprocal effects. *American Journal of Sociology, 87,* 1257–1286.

LaRocco, J. M., House, J. S., & French, J. R. J., Jr. (1980). Social support, occupational stress, and health. *Journal of Health and Social Behavior, 21,* 202–218.

Latham, G. P., & Saari, L. M. (1984). Do people do what they say. Further studies on the situational interview. *Journal of Applied Psychology, 69,* 569–573.

McClelland, G. H., & Judd, C. M. (1993). Statistical difficulties of detecting interactions and moderator effects. *Psychological Bulletin, 114,* 376–390.

Miller, R. G., Jr. (1966). *Simultaneous statistical inference.* New York: McGraw-Hill.

Mohr, G. (1986). *Die Erfassung psychischer Befindensbeeinträchtigungen bei Industriearbeitern* [Measuring disturbances of psychological well-being]. Frankfurt/Main, Germany: Peter Lang.

Motowidlo, S. J., & van Scotter, J. R. (1994). Evidence that task performance should be distinguished from contextual performance. *Journal of Applied Psychology, 79,* 475–480.

Neisser, U. (1982). *Memory observed: Remembering in natural contexts.* San Francisco: Freemann.

Nunnally, J. C. (1978). *Psychometric theory* (2nd ed.) New York: McGraw-Hill.

Organ, D. (1988). *Organizational citizenship behavior: The good soldier syndrome.* Lexington, MA: Lexington.

Pearce, J., Branyicki, I., & Bukacsi, G. (1994). Person-based reward systems: A theory of organizational reward practices in reform-communist organizations. *Journal of Organizational Behavior, 15,* 261–282.

Roth, P. L., Switzer, F. S., Campion, J. E., & Jones, S. D. (1994, July). *The impact of missing data in criterion related validation research.* Paper presented at the meeting of the Society for Industrial and Organizational Psychology, Nashville, TN.

Rotter, J. B. (1966). Generalized expectancies for internal versus external control of reinforcement. *Psychological Monographs, 80*(609).

Rotter, J. B. (1975). Some problems and misconceptions related to the construct of internal versus external control of reinforcement. *Journal of Consulting and Clinical Psychology, 43,* 56–67.

Sadri, G., & Robertson, I. T. (1993). Self-efficacy and work-related behaviour: A review and meta-analysis. *Applied Psychology: An International Review, 42,* 139–152.

Saks, A. M. (1995) Longitudinal field investigation of the moderating and mediating effects of self-efficacy on the relationship between training and newcomer adjustment. *Journal of Applied Psychology, 80,* 211–225.

Scheier, M. F., & Carver, C. S. (1985). Optimism, coping and health: assessment and implications of generalized outcome expectancies. *Health Psychology, 4,* 219–247.

Schwarzer, R., Bäßler, J., Kwiatek, P., Schröder, K., & Zhang, J. X. (1997). The assessment of optimistic self-beliefs: Comparison of the German, Spanish, and Chinese Versions of the General Self-Efficacy Scale. *Applied Psychology: An International Review, 46.*

Schultz-Gambard, J., & Altschuh, E. (1993). Unterschiedliche Führungsstile im geeinten Deutschland [Different leadership-styles in the unified Germany]. *Zeitschrift für Sozialpsychologie, 24*(3), 167–175.

Semmer, N. (1984). *Streßbezogene Tätigkeitsanalyse: Psychologische Untersuchungen zur Analyse von Streß am Arbeitsplatz* [Stress-oriented analysis of work: Psychological studies on the analysis of stress in the workplace]. Weinheim, Germany: Beltz.

Semmer, N., & Dunckel, H. (1991). Stressbezogene Arbeitsanalyse [Stress-oriented work analysis]. In S. Greif, E. Bamberg, & N. Semmer (Eds.), *Psychischer Stress am Arbeitsplatz* (pp. 57–90). Göttingen, Germany: Hogrefe.

Stone, E. F., & Hollenbeck, J. R. (1984). Some issues associated with the use of moderated regression. *Organizational Behavior and Human Performance, 34,* 195–213.

Stumpf, S. A., Brief, A. P., & Hartman, K. (1987). Self-efficacy expectations and coping with career-related events. *Journal of Vocational Behavior, 31,* 91–108.

Taylor, M. S., Locke, E. A., Lee, C., & Gist, M. E. (1984). Type A behavior and faculty research productivity: What are the mechanisms? *Organizational Behavior and Human Decision Processes, 34,* 402–418.

Van Maanen, J., & Schein, E. H. (1979). Toward a theory of organizational socialization. *Research in Organizational Behavior, 1,* 209–264.

Zapf, D. (1991). Streßbezogene Arbeitsanalyse bei der Arbeit mit unterschiedlichen Bürosoftwaresystemen [Stress-oriented job analysis of work with office software systems]. *Zeitschrift für Arbeits-und Organisationspsychologie, 35,* 2–14.

Zedeck, S. (1971). Problems with the use of "moderator" variables. *Psychological Bulletin, 76,* 295–310.

Made in the USA
San Bernardino,
CA

59092645R00073